Contents

M000192346

History of WritersCorps 5
Foreword 7
Introduction 9

1 Revolution of the Ordinary 13

Maiana Minahal 15
Kenneth F. Carroll 19
Ishle Yi Park 23
Jeffrey McDaniel 27
Melissa Tuckey 31
Elissa G. Perry 35
Beto Palomar 44
Aja Couchois Duncan 49
Monica A. Hand 56
D. Scot Miller 58

2 Dirty and Alive We Cried 61

Danielle Montgomery 63
marcos ramírez 67
Alison Seevak 71
Michele Kotler 75
Gamal Abdel Chasten 80
Chrissy Anderson-Zavala 87
Cathy Arellano 91
Paola Corso 100
Myron Michael Hardy 104
Kim Nelson 107

3 The Only War is the War Against the Imagination 111

Joel Dias-Porter (DJ Renegade) 113
Mahru Elahi 118
Thomas Centollela 124
Hoa Nguyen 128

Christopher Sindt *132*
Stephen Beachy *135*
Colette DeDonato *142*
Ryan Grim *145*
Joy Jones *147*
Katherine LeRoy *150*

4 Birthright *153*

Uchechi Kalu *163*
Will Power *167*
Judith Tannenbaum *171*
Kathy Evans *175*
John Rodriguez *179*
Seshat Yonshea Walker *183*
Livia Kent *187*
Leslie Davis *193*
Milta Ortiz *195*

5 The Shapes of Listening *199*

Ellis Avery *201*
Michelle Matz *206*
Michele Elliott *209*
Andrew Saito *213*
Mary "Maya" Hebert *216*
JoNelle Toriseva *220*
Barbara Schaefer *224*
Peter Money *227*
Cindy Je *231*
Chad Sweeney *237*

Acknowledgments 240
WritersCorps Teachers 240

Days I Moved
Through Ordinary Sounds

The Teachers of WritersCorps
in Poetry and Prose

Edited by Chad Sweeney

City Lights Foundation Books
San Francisco

Managing Editor: Melissa Hung
Editorial Assistant: Caitlyn O'Connell

Cover art © Jenifer K. Wofford
Book design by Linda Ronan

Library of Congress Cataloging-in-Publication Data

Days I moved through ordinary sounds : the teachers of WritersCorps in poetry
and prose / edited by Chad Sweeney.
      p. cm.
ISBN 978-1-931404-10-5
1. Teachers' writings, American. 2. American poetry—20th century. 3.
American poetry—21st century. 4. American literature—20th century. 5.
American literature—21st century. I. Sweeney, Chad. II. WritersCorps. III. Title.

PS591.T4D39 2009
810.8'0054—dc22

                         2008046624

The City Lights Foundation was formed with the goal of advancing deep
literacy, which is not only the ability to read and write but fluency in the
knowledge and skills that enable us to consciously shape our lives and the
life of our community. We believe that nurturing the ability to think critically,
to discern truth, and to communicate knowledge is essential to a democratic
society.

Visit our website: www. citylights.com

City Lights Foundation Books are published at the City Lights Bookstore,
261 Columbus Avenue, San Francisco, CA 94133

A History of WritersCorps

WritersCorps is a celebrated national program that brings creative writing into the lives of youth. Each year, hundreds of young people living in some of the nation's most economically disadvantaged neighborhoods experience firsthand the power of writing. WritersCorps' dedicated teaching artists, all published writers themselves, employ innovative curricula that makes literature relevant to the experiences of their students. With its award-winning publications and its popular reading series, WritersCorps has become a national arts and literacy model.

WritersCorps was born out of discussions between Jane Alexander, former chair of the National Endowment for the Arts (NEA), and Eli Siegel, then-director of AmeriCorps. Today, hundreds of writers have taught in their communities, inspiring youth and working diligently to create a safe place for young people to discover themselves through writing. WritersCorps teachers make lasting connections within their communities and become valued mentors and role models.

San Francisco, Washington, D.C., and Bronx, New York, were selected as the three sites for WritersCorps, chosen for these cities' exemplary art agencies with deep community roots and for their traditions of community activism among writers. In these three cities, WritersCorps' teaching artists, working at public schools and social service organizations, have helped young people of virtually every race, ethnicity and age improve their literacy and communication skills, while offering creative expression as an alternative to violence, truancy, alcohol and drug abuse.

In 1997, WritersCorps transitioned from a federally funded program to an independent alliance, supported by a collaboration of public and private partners. D.C. WritersCorps, Inc. is now a nonprofit organization, while the San Francisco and Bronx WritersCorps are projects of the San Francisco Arts Commission and the Bronx Council for the Arts, respectively. WritersCorps has developed a national structure administered by these three sites to provide greater cooperation and visibility, while at the same time encouraging the independence of each site to respond most effectively to its community.

To learn more about WritersCorps contact:

Bronx WritersCorps: 718-409-1265, www.bronxarts.org
D.C. WritersCorps: 202-332-5455, www.dcwriterscorps.org
San Francisco WritersCorps: 415-252-4655, www.writerscorps.org

Foreword

One week ago, Barack Obama was elected president of the United States.

Many of us have experienced epiphanic moments in the wake of this election. Mine came at Mount Hope Cemetery in Rochester, New York. I was in Rochester to read at a local community college. When I discovered that the grave of Frederick Douglass was ten minutes away, I asked my host to bring me there. Little did I realize that the grave of an escaped slave had become an altar.

Frederick Douglass lies beneath a stone slab inscribed with his name and the dates of birth and death. Scattered across the slab there were withered flowers, pennies, piles of acorns and stones, a tiny American flag. There was an Obama button carefully placed in the O in *Douglass*. There was a service employees union T-shirt—with an "I Voted Today" sticker—draped at the base of the tomb. There was a newspaper unfurled above the dates *1818-1895*. The headline said: *Obama Wins*.

Douglass believed so deeply in the power of the word that he published a newspaper in Rochester more than one hundred and sixty years ago to demand the abolition of slavery and the recognition of Black people as human beings. Now someone had left a newspaper at his grave with a headline that recalled the words of William Blake: "What is now proved was once only imagin'd."

The writers and teachers of WritersCorps embrace the same faith in the power of the word to revolutionize society, and this anthology is the proof. Their belief in literacy has sustained them and their students through the Illiterate Presidency of George Bush. They bring poems, stories and plays into so-called "non-traditional" settings, which are, in fact, the most traditional settings of all, given the communal origins of poetry, storytelling and theater. No doubt they have saved lives. This is not hyperbole.

These writer-teachers, and the communities they serve, reflect the rise of new voices in a new America. They are immigrants and the children of immigrants. They are the descendants of slaves. They elected Barack Obama.

The writers of WritersCorps represent the spirit of this society at its most generous. These writers exemplify the ideal of service to the community. We could even call them "community organizers" (insert Republican sneer here). Oh yes: They can also write. It is only fitting, after the WritersCorps writers have enabled so many of the damned and despised to find their voices, that they should speak for themselves in the pages of this anthology.

And how they speak, with compassion, intelligence and fire. The most striking characteristic of this collection, however, is the quality of fearlessness. These writers are unafraid to explore the most intimate details of their own experience; they are equally unafraid to take strong political stands on the great struggles of the day. They have a keen sense of history, paying homage to the grandfathers and grandmothers who labored in the fields before them; they have an equally sharp sense of the future, embodied by the students and communities they know so well. Again and again, there are manifestations of that faith in the power of the word to heal, console, redeem and transcend.

This anthology is more than a record of WritersCorps. It is a chronicle of our times. It is a newspaper fluttering on the tomb of an escaped slave.

Martín Espada
November 2008

Introduction

By Chad Sweeney

There is no single portrait one could paint of a WritersCorps teacher—avant-guardist, slam performer, comedian, gothic novelist, playwright, lyric poet, storyteller. *Days I Moved Through Ordinary Sounds* offers the range of the writing of these teaching artists, and in a parallel gesture, investigates the vision, commitment and practice of those who shared writing with young people in public schools, detention facilities, homeless shelters, and with newly arrived immigrants in San Francisco, Washington D.C. and the Bronx. "Poetry is not a luxury," according to Audre Lorde, "It is a vital necessity of our existence . . . [as] survival and change first made into language, then into idea, then into tangible action." In my seven years as a teaching artist in WritersCorps, I learned this not as an instrument of faith, but as hard fact, reinforced by daily witness in my own life, in classrooms and in community theaters. This collection celebrates the personal power we achieve through writing, a return to our birthright in language, and a transformation of the world—one student, one teacher, one writer at a time.

WritersCorps was born in 1994 out of the traditions of AmeriCorps, the National Endowment for the Arts and a long line of government-supported programs like Roosevelt's WPA which employed artists to teach and to produce significant literary work. San Francisco, Washington D.C., and the Bronx were chosen as the three WritersCorps sites because of the strong arts organizations in these cities. Jeffrey McDaniel, from that first year in Washington D.C., recalls "the camaraderie with other writers, the fertile energy of this dynamic group of beautiful, poetry-crazed lunatics." In the fifteen years of the program's life, more than 250 writers have worked with thousands of young people: youth who live in economically disadvantaged neighborhoods; who have recently immigrated to the United States, often into cramped spaces with distant relatives; who are struggling to maintain the sense of self through a period of incarceration. WritersCorps teachers create innovative lessons to make literature relevant by meeting the youth where they are, and by providing platforms for these under-represented voices to be heard, through award-winning publications and reading series.

The writers gathered here discuss their process and inspiration, and many point out that teaching with WritersCorps was a turning point in their careers, as it both expanded their artistic vision and solidified their relationship with community. They saw words transformed into action. Chris Sindt, who went on to direct the creative writing program at St. Mary's College, tells us that WritersCorps "provided urgency and specificity to some vague notions I had about social engagement." Maiana Minahal taught for WritersCorps before becoming the director of June Jordan's revered program, Poetry for the People, at U.C. Berkeley. She recalls: "I was changed, as a teacher and as a person, by working with the many homeless youth, young women, teen moms and first generation immigrant children . . . who came to internalize the belief that they couldn't write, or that their stories weren't important." Milta Ortiz's journey mirrors those of many of her students at Mission High, as she describes coming to the U.S. from war-torn El Salvador at the age of eight. "When I learned that my mother's uncle in El Salvador was murdered for sharing political ideas . . . I would never again take lightly my ability to formulate a critical opinion."

Teaching is not martyrdom. I often hear people say, "Oh it's wonderful, that you're willing to work with *those kids*." What I believe these people miss is that teaching is not a one-way vector of giving, but an exchange—not even a circle, but a circle of circles. Every WritersCorps teacher gathers a different montage of experiences, but one common refrain is that the work is surprisingly rewarding. I was privileged to teach for WritersCorps in schools in the Mission District of San Francisco and in a housing project near "Crack Alley." My theories about humanity were quickly hammered flat to make a table for us to sit around and write together and share our stories. We nurtured one another with our presence and with language, and I have never felt more complete. Novelist Ellis Avery explains, "Writing in community gathers us around the proverbial campfire and reminds us why we do this: because hearing stories helps us make sense of the world. Because telling them helps us make sense of ourselves." Aja Couchois Duncan testifies, "It was in *writing through it* that those young people taught me something I will carry always: sometimes the most we can do is to show up for ourselves, for one another." This *showing up* Duncan speaks of is not an easy matter, as the real human work is not a flash of heroism, but a daily dedication to being awake, sensitive, available for the people around us.

Days I Moved Through Ordinary Sounds gathers the essence of these experiences together in the writings of fifty energetic teaching art-

ists—from that first year in 1994 to the present, where a new genera-
tion of WritersCorps teachers, like Milta Ortiz, has entered the field. I
am happy to report the field is expanding, through WritersCorps and
programs like it all over America. These pages celebrate the extraordi-
nary commitment and ability of writers who have chosen to live in the
world and to serve it with their hands and with their words.

Revolution of the Ordinary

Maiana Minahal

When I immigrated from the Philippines to the U.S. as a child, I quickly realized that one of my most important tasks was learning to master the English language—my daily currency. While I worked hard at school to gain sophistication in English and to lose my "accent," at home I began to understand less and less of my own parents' conversations. I lost native fluency in the languages I was born with—both my family's dialect (Cebuano Visayan) and the Philippine language (Tagalog). I came to a complicated appreciation of the power of language(s), and my writing springs from this paradox: how language both holds the power to communicate and create a shared understanding of humanity, as well as to silence or rend the possible connections between people.

WritersCorps was a turning point for me—my first teaching experiences after college—before I went on to direct Poetry for the People and to lecture at U.C. Berkeley. Those first WritersCorps classes gave me a place to attempt, as bell hooks says in *Teaching to Transgress*, "(t)o educate as the practice of freedom." I hoped to cultivate my students' creative and liberatory thinking, while sharpening their writing skills. I'd tell my students that in building construction, the builders are limited by the materials at their disposal, by the kind of rock, metal and wood available—whereas writers, in building texts, are limited only by the words they know and, more importantly, by their imaginations.

I was changed, as a teacher and as a person, by working with the many homeless youth, young women, teen moms and first generation immigrant children who were my students at Central City Hospitality House, the Center for Young Women's Development, and Career Resources Development Center in San Francisco. These were youth who were labeled "at-risk," who came to internalize the belief that they couldn't write, or that their stories weren't important. None of them came to writing easily, yet they didn't give up. With each poem they struggled to create, they showed me honest examples of what it really means to own the power of language, to be socially engaged writers—and I thank them for that.

You Bring Out the Filipina in Me

after Sandra Cisneros

you bring out the filipina in me
the language born of blood in me
the *p* instead of *f* in me
the glottal catch in me
the visayan the tagalog in me
the ancestors in me

you bring out
the murder of magellan in me
the revolution of seven thousand islands in me
to survive 500 years of colonizers in me

you bring out the guerrilla soldier in me
the olonggapo bar hostess in me
the mail order bride in me

you bring out the *bahala na* immigrant in me
the *god they're so american* in me
the *yes, i do speak english* in me
the tnt green card in me

you bring out the pinay in me
the sass in me smartass badass in me
the proud walker shit talker
third world girl the majority in me

you bring out the barkada in me
wolf among sheep in me
the danger the desire in me
the drink til i'm drunk
fuck til i'm good and fucked

you bring out the queer in me
the dyke in me
the brave beautiful butch in me
voracious femme in me
the *bastos* the *bakla*
the *walang hiya* in me

you bring out the wake up

laughing laughing
not crying
in me
my brother
my brother
mahal mahal kita
yes you do
oh yes you do

———

bahala na – "what god wills"
barkada – friends
bastos – rude; bakla – faggot
walang hiya – shameless
mahal kita – i love you

Ordinary

Our honeyed tongues elude the rib of words
that could climb into open sky
or choke us like a pillar of salt.

We've approached flight before.
Found it too unguarded.
That gem whose absence hadn't yet wounded

decades ago, when as a girl I hopscotched
under magnolia tree shade, next to the house on Samar Avenue—
and as a girl, oceans away, you might have pressed palms
        against a glass window,

perched in the back seat of a car crawling the crumbling road to
        San Salvador.
I can almost picture you, years later, navigating the corridors of a
        strange university,
suddenly in the land of Clorox and strip malls.

In what cities since then did we pack suitcases with filings of
grief, airplane across time zones between tropics and tundra?
When did we decide to shave down our wings?

Poem for Alegria

sometimes i think
i want to say
you a honeysuckle smell
on a hot hot day / n
you the sculpture come from
a wet bar of clay / n
you a new love letter
every day of the week! / n
you a song song sonata
i got to keep singing
can't help but be singing

n then again
i think
you more
you a operatic orchestration
a movement in the key of "a"
a symphonic suite of arias that start
alegria
alegria
alegria

you the pure pool of water
cool rain leaves
you low rumbling thunder
rolling along the sea
you strong strong for speaking / n
i want to say
you living breathing dancing singing
you flame fire earth
you a song song sonata
i got to sing

Maiana Minahal was born in Manila, raised in Los Angeles, and now lives in the San Francisco Bay Area. At U.C. Berkeley she lectured and served as director of Poetry for the People. She received her M.F.A. from Antioch University and is the author of the poetry chapbooks *closer* and *Sitting Inside Wonder*. Civil Defense Poetry will publish a collection of her poetry, *Legend of Sondayo*, in 2009.

Kenneth F. Carroll

My writing and service began with my mother, who believed that true charity was giving when you yourself may not have much—like sharing a few slices of bread with a neighbor when you are down to your last loaf. So writing and service were never separate acts for me. This was later affirmed when I read writers like Frederick Douglass, Amiri Baraka, June Jordan, James Baldwin, Lucille Clifton, Gaston Neal and hundreds of others who believed that their art carried with it the responsibility of witness-bearing and advocacy. WritersCorps provided a structure and form to a service I had begun years before when I used up my vacation and sick leave from my corporate job to go into Washington D.C. schools, prisons and community centers to conduct readings and workshops. WritersCorps' greatness is in its ability to provide an opportunity for hundreds of writers to use their art in service to others. Its greatness is also exemplified by the thousands of new writers it has helped to create, a generation of young people who have defined themselves as artists and activists. As my mother knew, sharing does not require riches—only that we see ourselves in each other.

Painting of Frederick Douglass, 2nd Floor Charles Hart Middle School

"It is easier to build a strong child than to repair a broken man."
—Frederick Douglass

The hallway patiently waits, yearns
for the meticulous brush of janitors
scraping away the vestiges of
children who do not understand

that they are the protagonists
in a centuries-old drama full
of monsters and circumstances
waiting to devour them.

Frederick Douglass is tacked high
above the fray of their precarious

lives, he looks down upon them sternly
furrowed brow in etched face

trying to convince them that the even-
second-rate education they despise
might still be sanctuary, like his education
of wielded whips & wrested words.

I tutor the 7th grader who cannot spell
"cool," does not know the name of the
continent where Frederick Douglass'
mother was stolen from, the bad

light-skinned boy, who I have reluctantly
let back into the program, asks me if
he should put down the name of his
murdered father on his permission slip.

I think of Douglass, young boy, motherless,
father a mystery—perhaps any white man with
slaves. I think of the children who fill these halls
with sound to keep the drone of their uncertain

futures from drowning out their laughter. I wonder
if they ever look up at the face looking down at them
if they ever remember, wide-eyed, beautiful, endangered,
"that reading makes a man unfit for slavery."

Poetry Club
for Nikki

a woman is yelling from a doorway,
august lingers like the smell of burning wire,
she is admonishing children who are not hers
"get off that tree, they planted it for the dead girl"

I wonder if this tree will live long enough
to be baptized in a dc thunderstorm
or provide shade for the weary at the bus stop

this sapling, named after the girl you murdered,
reminds me of your first poem
full of promise, in need of care

I looked for that poem
when I got the news
all sudden & sideways
& easy to doubt

not like the movies, where an old white dude
with a calm modulated voice asks you to sit down
instead a 15-year-old blurts out this horror
launching it abruptly into my brain without
count down or build up "Nikki killed dat girl"

I hold myself together with feigned ignorance
wishing to have no knowledge of a language
capable of conveying the story of a butcher knife
plunged into the future of a 14-year-old by a
13-year-old

but the young voice thwarts my retreat
into this mirage of denial, wants to know
when the poetry club will start again
as if there is a poem big enough to fill the
gaping hole that has produced this obscene absence

I watch you walk again for the first time
into my workshop, hands on bouncing, narrow
hips, eyes already rolling without provocation
you pretending not to listen but refusing to
leave, your smile a scrim for your anger

looking for your poem, I find your picture
I want to run to the court where you are being arraigned,
insist that the judge examine your smile & imagination,
demand that they be declared exculpatory evidence

but he will show me this tree,
this thin frightened maple, its root
fertilized with blood & a grandmother's tears
bearing the name of a dc holocaust victim

I remember how you snatched your poem from me
your response to my compliment, you hop-scotching
between rage & joyous innocence
the 15-year-old wants me to believe
that you would have traded that knife for a pen
that behind all that sucking of teeth & attitude
was a poet's face trying to recognize itself

When are we going to start the poetry club again?
I hear between the pulsing migraine of words
that tell me you are a murderer, that repeat a
mantra louder than a February chorus of I've
Known Rivers, "Nikki killed dat girl"

I long for the belief of zealots & new lovers,
wish that I could believe in the ability of words
to replace embraces, could believe that children
sent to or left to be swallowed by despair on this
side of the river, can choose life & art when
death & destruction are more potent & available

I remember how you returned your poem to me
crumbled up like hardening snow
unleashed from your fist onto my desk,
its only edit, your signature & an august
thunderstorm gathering above your smile

Kenneth F. Carroll directed the D.C. WritersCorps from 1995 to 2008 and is the author of the poetry collection *So What: For the White Dude Who Said This Ain't Poetry*. His work has appeared widely in such places as the *Washington Post* and *Bum Rush the Page: A Def Poetry Jam*. Three of his plays have been produced: *The Mask, Make My Funk the P-Funk* and *Walking To Be Free*. He has written for BET Television and for independent film, including the award-winning documentary *Voices Against Violence*, winner of the Rosebud Award.

© Ishle Yi Park

Ishle Yi Park

WritersCorps gave me the opportunity to work with students from many countries in the English as a Second Language classes at Newcomer High School. It was wonderful to work with young people who still reveled in the beauties of language, who discovered new words in their pocket dictionaries daily, and who helped me rediscover the sheer terror and joy and work involved in creative writing. In WritersCorps, I was part of a community of socially engaged and politically conscious writers, each of us doing our part to nurture a younger generation of artists. Often as a writer, one feels alone in the universe, so it is important to feel connected to a larger sphere of artists for moral and spiritual support. Teaching creative writing is a humbling, exhausting and rewarding experience. It has taught me about the circle of life, and the importance of giving back.

My own writing ranges from autobiographical prose to lyric poetry. I write about Korean Americans, love, and struggle. I write to make sense of my worlds and to try to envision new ones. In an essay entitled "Rootedness: The Ancestor as Foundation," Toni Morrison wrote, "It seems to me that the best art is unquestionably political and irrevocably beautiful at the same time." With each poem or story I write, I am trying to capture those essential, indescribable, yet crucial moments in the lives of working-class Korean Americans, and to try to attain a balance between politics and beauty in my own art. I write in the attempt to create positive, moving and honest art that can be appreciated by all audiences. Eric Gamalinda has a poem that ends, "be beautiful, brief, and blinding." I used to write in the hope of achieving this dream; now I write because I simply cannot imagine life without it. It's as necessary as prayer, or faith.

Looking back, teaching with WritersCorps was a beautiful experience. I was in my early twenties, living in Oakland, performing poetry, and teaching 24/7. This was before *Def Poetry Jam*, before becoming the poet laureate of Queens, before the hoopla and madness that comes from being a full-time artist. Maybe life was more honest then: less grandeur, more grind, more grit, more everyday grace.

Jejudo Dreams

In Jejudo, there are women who have dived for generations,
scalloping shells off coral reefs
to support their weak, spendthrift husbands
and sustain the island life. These women,
seal smooth with black river hair tied thick
into a bun, will, even nine months pregnant,
hold their breath and submerge.

In Queens, I read about them
as if they were not a part of my mother's memory,
as if she never once loved their indecipherable accents
thick with the knowledge of water
in a time when wet laundry still slapped on rock—
they skirted her Daegu reality.

and I'm drowning in the land to which she swam,
cuz when I try to speak my homelanguage, my tongue
flops in my mouth like a dying fish:
desperate, silver, and shining with effort.
These fish line my parents' store shelves,
invade our dreams in huge, peeled-skin schools,
their sour, two-day old smell clings to my mother's
woolen sweaters and my father's corduroy pants,
to the dusk of their skin as they watch television.

This smell was my shame growing up,
my secret; the reason I took three showers a day,
got dropped off a block away from school
so the Whitestone kids would never know
that my father drove the puke-green van
smelling of fish, so they would never wrinkle
their noses at me and say I smelled like fish,
or dirty women. For fifteen years, I crossed my legs,
washed, prayed, hid.

I erased my mother's memories
and replaced them with rote school texts,
learned to be ashamed of my parents,
their accent, to interpret their hard-earned smell
as stink, to think diamond-cut eyes undesirable,

some of us trying to Anglicize them
with Elmer's glue or cosmetic surgery . . .

My dongsengs: what are we doing if not quietly, desperately
    drowning?
Who is here to teach us how to swim?

I want to know those Jejudo women
beyond their slick, oceanic frame—
if pollution from Seoul mars their skin,
    if broken shells shrapnel their callused palms,
      if their thighs are as smooth and tight
        as taut silk, if their hair ever danced
          with locks of fresh seaweed,
            like the lyrics of songs they sing after work,
              lyrics of songs they hear underwater,
        if their husbands ever beat them,
      how they cry, how they laugh,
        how they fight,
          the mottled, murky bayous and lagoons
          of their dreams.

How it feels . . . to hold your breath so long
your lungs, on the verge of burst, steel themselves
while you grab, wrench, take what you need more than air,
    and break the surface . . .

There are times when I trivialize these desires,
but at night, I wonder: will my ancestors not hear me when I die?
Will they mistake me for a white bakwai ghost
because of my accent? Will all the history I embody
unravel with my time because this tongue
cannot recall the words braided into my bloodline?

These women, who are my women,
    these songs, which are my songs . . .

In Jejudo, there are women
who have dived for generations,

    they are calling me back to myself,
      the truest, rough coral of myself,

I take a deep breath—

and go fish.

Railroad

One day I will write a poem
about my father as a mountain,
and there will be no shame for the dynamite
and the blasted hole, the pickaxes and steam drills
paving their own resolute path,
for the railroad ploughed through his core,
for shattered rocks, for pungent scent of pines.
My father will be a mountain surrounded by wind
that wears him down as slowly as marriage,
as America, as time. But he is still
a man and a mountain: drilled, hammered, alive,
unaware of all who love him from the far track.

Ishle Yi Park is the first woman to become poet laureate of Queens, New York. Her book, *The Temperature of This Water*, received three literary awards, including the PEN/Beyond Margins Award. She has appeared on HBO's *Def Poetry Jam* and her work has been published widely, including in *The Best American Poetry 2003*, *Ploughshares*, *New American Writing* and *Century of the Tiger: One Hundred Years of Korean Culture in America*.

Jeffrey McDaniel

My two years with D.C. WritersCorps (1994-96) came at the perfect time—I had just finished grad school at George Mason and was looking for something useful and poetry-related to do. What I remember most is the camaraderie with other writers, the fertile energy of this dynamic group of beautiful, poetry-crazed lunatics that director Kenny Carroll nurtured. As a writer and thinker, it was invigorating to bounce between the world of my M.F.A. program, where people in workshop wondered if poems were "too linear," and where "accessible" was a putdown—and the world of WritersCorps, where the poems you brought into workshop had to be accessible if you were going to captivate and hopefully inspire a population that wasn't fluent in the coded maneuvers of contemporary poetry.

My WritersCorps sites were Clean and Sober Streets, a rehab for homeless people within a large homeless shelter; CADAC, a rehab facility based at St. Elizabeths in Southeast; and the Mount Pleasant Library. At Clean and Sober Streets, I worked on an oral history project transcribing the bottoms of various recovering addicts. The Mount Pleasant Library workshop had a small but loyal following consisting of local poets I respected, including Jose Padua and Heather Davis, who began dating in the workshop and are now happily married. At CADAC, the poetry workshop was the only place in the locked facility where men and women could be in the same room without professional supervision. Some exciting work was produced there, but I did have to make sure people kept their fingertips to themselves under the table.

In many ways, WritersCorps planted seeds in me that didn't fully bloom until a few years later when I moved to Los Angeles and conducted workshops at a variety of high schools. For three consecutive years I independently rag-tag assembled six high school poets to participate in Brave New Voices, the National Teen Poetry Slam. How powerful it was to see poetry become an active, positive force in a young person's life. WritersCorps taught me that just because a blueprint doesn't exist and you're not completely sure what you're doing doesn't mean you still can't dive in and make something happen.

Day 4305

Eleven years, three months sober, I enter a liquor store
    to buy a pack of chewing gum for a friend

and find myself surrounded by bottles filled with liquid
    that can kill me, like inside each one there's a switch

that could unfreeze the drunkard within. The drunkard is on ice.
    To him it's still December 6th, 1993.

We've just stumbled out of the Fox and Hounds Bar in Dupont
    Circle, a half-dozen thimbles of whisky rattling

in our guts. We're jabbing the key into the car, igniting
    the engine. The cops have not swooped in

and yanked us out yet. The drunkard in me kicks my ribs.
    He can smell the Old Grand Dad on the shelf.

He wants to slug eggshells of bourbon till our nerve endings
    are as dull as the butter knives in a psych ward.

He remembers scurrying through the brain's elaborate hallways,
    holding a fire extinguisher filled with Jim Beam

and squelching all the thoughts smoldering inside.
    The drunkard laughs at the list of places we've passed out:

the East Village stairwell, the Philadelphia train yard,
    behind the wheel of a one-eyed Pinto, in the arms

of Lila Shepherd, in the legs of Melissa Browne. The drunkard
    laughs about snorting 4 grams of coke on an empty stomach

and puking so hard I ripped out the lining of my throat
    like the velvet sleeve of a tuxedo. The drunkard

could care less that we were an unemployed loser, that our penis
    had shriveled into a limp parachute chord, something

we tugged on each night, when the drugs wore off,
    and we plummeted back to earth, hoping

it would ease the crash. I was in San Diego a few years back:
    9 a.m., a hot Saturday morning, jogging this palm-tree path,

parallel to the Pacific, water shimmering, when I noticed
    this old bum in an overcoat conked out

on a patch of grass, the bottle in its brown paper nightgown
    balanced in his palm, all these chipper, go-getter

Yuppies putzing past him in their day-glo running gear.
    And it hit me—the old bum with his crowbar of a smile,

that's the oblivion I was seeking, to be so supremely blotto
    I could pass out on a sunny morning, my whole body

splayed like a fuck you to their way of life. A guy
    enters the store, grabs Grandpa by the throat.

If I live this life 100 more times, 98 times I die drunk. I enter
    the windshield and don't come out, heroin's cherubs

seal their chubby palms over my lips. The street dealer
    in North Philly with the switchblade slices my face

open like a papaya. Last week they found Hilary balled-up
    in a bathroom. Before that it was Raymond in the desert,

a telescope jabbed into his forearm and a tube looping
    from his exhaust pipe to his lips. On every leaf

of every branch of my family tree, I see this illness, this hunger
    that multiplies when you feed it, this octopus

expanding in the belly. I haven't used in 11 years, and still it runs
    through me. I fall asleep, he's running laps around

my pelvis. I wake, and he's churning up my calves, already
    broken a sweat. How do you beat an opponent

that works-out more than you do, that has no weakness?
    Sam said there'd be moments like this,

when the only thing between me and a drink was a god
    I'm not sure I believe in. I grab the pack

of gum, go to the counter. *Anything else?* the guy asks.
    A swimming pool overflowing with vodka? Crack

rocks the size of softballs? A sand box filled with crystal
    meth? I am the miracle. I am the hand reaching

out of the wreck. I don't care if it's true. It's what I need
    to tell myself to make it out the door alive.

The Offer

I want to locate a bit of you, cradle it,
say: this, there is no word for this.

But they will. They who name everything
will define our actions
as we auction our bodies off to sleep.

In our single dream we'd compose
a manifesto on the irregularity of scars.

The very idea demands preparation, as if
choosing a school for an angel.

There are no angels. Just those things
blinking like the teeth of jackals
around the moon's significant tremble.

Isolate the idea of shaking our bodies
under the blank comfort of down and tell
me which way will our knuckles face?

Now shake the idea of our isolated bodies
as the sheets become our Miro.

If you stay, the walls will admit their cracks.
See it forming, already on their lips.

Jeffrey McDaniel is the author of four poetry books: *The Endarkenment* (University of Pittsburgh Press), and from Manic D Press, *The Splinter Factory, The Forgiveness Parade* and *Alibi School.* His work has appeared widely, including in *The Best American Poetry 1994* and *Ploughshares.* He teaches creative writing at Sarah Lawrence College.

Melissa Tuckey

I believe in the importance of poetry, in its power to engage heart and mind and encourage readers to appreciate the complexities of truth. For me this is a political thing. We have to find a new way of doing commerce, one that doesn't involve war. Poets have a responsibility to find language to describe the times in which we live and to give words to whatever is at stake. When there is silence, the poet must go in and find words. Politicians are happy to give us words and to name things, but too often the naming they do is the kind of double speak that George Orwell warned against: "war is peace, freedom is slavery, ignorance is strength." Poets steal our language back. They give us the power of imagination when imagination fails. Many of America's youth live in a world not depicted in mainstream media or in any other venue—but poetry, and programs like WritersCorps, give them the tools to make their voices heard.

Walking through the doors for the first time at Ron Brown Middle School in Southeast D.C. was a bit of a shock. The metal detectors, barred windows and bathrooms without toilet paper bore no resemblance to the suburban schools I attended growing up. When late spring hit, the classroom in which I taught had the only air conditioner on the third floor, so students from other classes crowded into the room for relief. There were months when the whole student body was not allowed to go outside during lunchtime as punishment for what a few trouble-makers had done. Class was often interrupted by the principal asking, "Would you behave this way at home?"

In spite of all of this, the school was bursting with poets, and the teacher I worked with, Ms. Anita Gay, was an inspiration, with a quiet yet powerful presence. Her seventh-grade students were memorizing poetry and writing and directing plays. I was thrilled when they came to me with notebooks full of poetry! Their passion for speaking their truth and their belief that the world should be fair was inspiring. From their fire and fearless imagination, I learned to take more risks in my own writing. I was impressed by what natural poets they are—fiercely committed to truth-telling, often on subjects the rest of the world is trying to ignore. I believe that if such talent and imagination are encouraged—anything is possible, not just in nurturing youth writing, but in nurturing a more hospitable world.

Portrait Of Mona Lisa In Palestine

Someone's erased her jawbone again
better she have no jaw at all
than a prominent chin

They say the sea's too restless
the horizon too full of promise

They've given her a drab background
and pocket of crushed cigarettes   Taken
away her veranda—replaced

the valley with a prison courtyard
Laughter used to rise from her mouth like birds
Fish leapt at the sound of her voice

Now they paint her mouth closed
They can't stand
the way she looks at them

II.

Late sunlight   olive grove   grave of her mother

Curators worry the mask is cracking

Beneath it all kinds of things we wouldn't want to know

She shouldn't have left the house for water

He shouldn't have gone to school that day

They shouldn't   let their kids play   in front of the Mosque

She shouldn't   have stood up to   that bulldozer

Who threw the rock? Why'd she mouth off?

Did somebody   move   in front of my gun?

III.

She wears no jewels

The dictionary says that rape
is the pumice
of grapes a turnip
a forage crop for sheep

rapture is rape
by God

God is occupant
in a theater
and you can add "of war"
to any sentence

thunderbolt of war
maidenflowerhead of war

heroics the opposite
of hysterics—

Re: The Acquittal of Salvadorian Generals

This afternoon I saw
a snowman
duct-taped
to a lawn chair sunbathing

    and the generals

argued
they weren't in control
of their men

time pulled a curtain
between justice and the crime

In front of the church a holy ghost

made of snow
beseeches

four dead nuns

rosary of human heads
in hand

there are no limits
for what they will do

Melissa Tuckey is the author of the poetry chapbook *Rope As Witness* (Pudding House Publications). Her poems have appeared in *Verse Daily, Beloit Poetry Journal, Painted Bride Quarterly, Poet Lore, Southeast Review* and elsewhere. She is the recipient of fellowships from Washington, D.C. Commission on the Arts and Humanities, Ohio Arts Council and a residency at Blue Mountain Center. She serves as co-director for Split This Rock Poetry Festival in Washington D.C. and is the events coordinator for D.C. Poets Against the War.

© Katharine Gin

Elissa G. Perry

" . . . don't worry, I make up all the parts that are true." — Nancy Boutilier (from *On the Eighth Day Adam Slept Alone*)

In August of 1977 our second-grade class at St. Louis Cathedral Elementary School was assigned the task of writing about our respective summer vacations. I asked if the story had to be true. It was when Miss Blaze said "no," that I began a journey of discovering and communicating truth through fiction. Already I did not fit neatly into what was supposed to define a newly middle-class, mid-western Black girl who was the daughter of firsts—first to integrate a neighborhood lunch counter, first to integrate a local professional college and first in the family to graduate college. A burgeoning love of language became my tool to write myself into new realities and new ways of being. At first I inserted myself into stories I heard my parents' acquaintances tell in line at the bank or the grocery store or the post office. I went hang gliding in California. I skipped rocks across a river in West Africa and ate goat stew in Iran. Later, I learned to find my own story and to know others through theirs—written or spoken; read, heard or witnessed. When we know someone's story, it's hard to judge and ridiculous to hate. I tell stories because they have to be told, otherwise they collect and fester in our common gut.

WritersCorps has been an influential experience in my life as large and relevant as that simple "no" twenty years before. To say that I "taught" at Ida B. Wells and McAteer High Schools would leave out so much of the experience. WritersCorps is where my passions for the written word and social justice first came together, not in theory, not in a book but in the actions of everyday life. When these young people wrote themselves into existence and then importance in their own minds and in the minds of each other—when Dameon, who had never written a word in his life, had filled his composition book and asked for another and then another; when Drummer asked how he could learn to spell better; when Vendetta wrote that she had too much respect for herself to keep living how she'd been living; when Tameka told me she'd found her imagination after weeks of insisting otherwise—something shifted that could not be shifted back. The power of language did the work.

From the novel *Ephemeris*

Becoming Darla 1979

I had three toys when I was growing up and it was these three toys I kept each time we moved. A Baby Alive, a Wiffle ball set and a set of Lincoln Logs. It got so my mother didn't have to ask which three toys I wanted to take when we packed up for the next rest stop. Her answer was always the same.

"A smart decision—a balanced array," she would say indicating the small lot with her KOOL Superlong. My mother liked to use words like array and meander, juxtapose and evoke. They were princess words and she fancied herself a princess.

"Listen to you, Janine!" Whenever we were in St. Louis my grandfather would smile and puff up with pride and humility at his educated daughter. He was a fascinated devotee of words and numbers but he himself had never attended school past eighth grade. That he made it that far, must have been an accomplishment. His graduation was one of the stories in his frequent refrain.

I wondered what she meant by "balanced array." Was it the indoor-outdoor toy thing or that one toy drew girl friends, one toy brought boy friends and the other drew both or neither? I liked the Baby Alive cause you could feed her applesauce and have it come out of the other end. When we were on the road I would use napkins from fast food restaurants for diapers. When we got to the next town, Baby Alive would be my Litmus Test (a Janine word). I liked to eat the applesauce out of the other end of Baby Alive. I had discovered this on a dry hot afternoon with breezes reminiscent of opening oven doors. The applesauce was still vaguely cool from the refrigerator and fruity and light.

Any girl I could convince to do this with me could be my friend. Not all girls were faced with this challenge. I knew something about this act was unusual. It would bind us in a secret society outside the rest of the bland landscape. Janine didn't know this. If she had ever asked why Danielle or Charlotte or Crystal didn't come around again, I might have told her but she didn't ask and I didn't tell.

Wiffle ball was a different thing altogether. I'd hit the ball directly into the boy who had pitched it. It didn't do damage but it stung. Boys thought I was tough, but if they'd been able to look closely, they'd have known I was all underbelly thinly disguised. We were rarely in one place long enough for anyone to figure out my unconscious rouse. I hit all the boys except Hank. Hank was not a boy though he was a man. Janine said he was a shiffless nigga when it was just she and me. When there were other grown folks around, Hank was an intellectual. He had been to college and all over the world. If gin and tonics were around, Hank was also a fabulous lover. He was my favorite Dad and Janine my only mother.

He had a blue station wagon with wood paneling, a nappy beard and a love for country music.

"Black people don't listen to country music, Hank," Janine said one time interrupting the rhythm of highway seams, Johnny Cash and wheat fields.

"Either Black people listen to country music or I ain't Black." He sounded like Bo Duke on the Dukes of Hazzard.

There was no doubting his hue and I had surmised that liking Janice Joplin was OK too.

"You've got to remember where you come from but you've also got to open up your world" he said to the rear view mirror. He knew the little girl was listening. He winked. I smiled. I liked the sound of that.

"You've got to broaden your horizons, Baby." Hank looked over at Janine and put his hand on her thigh but all she gave him was profile as she stared at the long flat road before them.

That time Wichita had been behind us, Denver in front. Leaving or going to, I still wasn't sure. Denver would be the first place I wouldn't be ready to leave. We stayed there 10 months. Down the street from Rosa Martinez. Rosa was Mexican.

"What are you?" she'd asked me after side-glancing my Baby Alive and rolling her eyes. She was a year and a half older than me and uninterested in the brown plastic doll.

"I'm Black." I told her wondering why she would ask such a stupid question. I noticed Rosa was getting breasts and felt the heat and tightness crawling up from my chest and spreading across my face for proposing we play with a doll.

"You must got something else in you with eyes like that. And look at your hair. It's straight and nappy at the same time. Girl, you just all mixed up."

She finished braiding her hair in the mirror. It shone against the white of her T-shirt. I could see the lace of her bra. "Come here. Let me do yours." She sat me down in front of the mirror and stood behind me. My one braid was as big as Rosa's forearm. My eyes were teeny compared to Rosa's big round ones. I didn't think Rosa would be my friend. I shrank down into my sternum but couldn't leave just yet.

"Sit up, girl. You gonna get a hunch in your back like some old lady." Rosa tapped my shoulder with the brush. I was her doll.

* * *

Hank's car was always dusty but I liked it that way. He didn't mind if I got ice cream on the back seat. He seemed to enjoy going to the gas station to clean it out. He moved the books from the backseat to the way back in neat stacks. Leroi Jones, Nella Larsen, Lao Tsu, Fyodor Doestoyevsky.

"Who are all of these people, Hank?" Rosa wasn't afraid to ask. She licked her chocolate ice cream from its pink plastic spoon. She filled up all of the senses and I couldn't control myself. Before I knew it, I had pinched her.

"Ow, quit it, punk." Rosa smacked my arm away. "So who are they?" Rosa sucked another spoonful.

Hank backed out of the car.

His ashy legs bent under baggy brown shorts. "They are people, young lady, people like you and me who have things to teach us as they learn, things they want to share."

"Hmph," Rosa turned her back to the books and leaned against the side of the car. "I like listening to music better than books and they got a lot of things to say too."

"Yes, they do, Rosa. There are lots of ways to communicate in the world." Hank looked at Rosa in a friendly way I did not like. Hank was mine and Rosa was mine and the two of them could not be friends. We would have to walk for ice cream from then on. I didn't tell Rosa she had dust on her behind from the side of the car.

"Let's go to my house." Rosa said as they pulled into the carport.

"Can I, Hank?"

"I don't know can you?" He sang into the rear view.

"May I?" I corrected myself.

"Yes, you may." He smiled and continued to watch me from the mirror.

"Thanks, Hank!" It seemed a mile from the middle of the backseat to the door and I couldn't get out fast enough. I slammed the door in my haste and then paused for a nanosecond waiting for Hank to say something about abusing the equipment but, he drove away. I hadn't noticed that the engine was still running when my dingy sneakers found their place on the parched pavement and I didn't stop to wonder where he was going.

I remembered those moments when movement had meant freedom. I was awake and unencumbered and six. Hank would take me driving on country roads. I would sit on his lap and steer. I was safe with him. We raced into the terrain. The toothy grill of the wood paneled station wagon chasing an invisible destination. We digested the dips and crests. Dust spread behind us a temporary marker of where we'd been.

"Yee haw!" He would holler as we bumped over the earth like a fast moving boat over waves. By human terms it was deserted, but in reality that desert was just a sleeping giant barely on the other side of the mountains. That day it awoke and swallowed him up whole.

"Where's Hank?" I didn't have to go past the kitchen to know that he wasn't there. The music was always on when Hank was home. Janine was sitting at the table in silence with a KOOL and a drink.

"Out." Was her only response.

"What's for dinner?" I ventured another question.

"Whatever it is you decide to make."

I knew to stop my inquiries and left Janine to her anesthetizing (that's what she called it).

That was the first night of waiting for Hank to come home.

* * *

And we waited. There was always that sense of waiting. Not of suspense but of suspension. Being held in limbo for some unknown destiny. Anxious for it's unfolding.

Eight more months we stayed. I finished out the school year before we packed up again. I gave up my Baby Alive for some books that Hank had left. Janine decided that two books equals one toy. I chose *The Member of the Wedding* (Hank had said that I reminded him of the girl in the story) and *Invisible Man* (I just liked the sound of it) and they were infinitely more than one toy.

"Mom, when are we going to stop?" I continued looking out of the window at the screenplay flickering by. I could only gather anything meaningful by focusing on the distance. A barn. A mountain. A haystack in a field.

"Why, you hungry already?" Janine looked over her shoulder before changing lanes. My mother looked quick and harried but there was no one around and no where for us to be.

"No. I just mean . . . I don't know. You know. Like where I can go to one school and stuff." I was afraid to continue. This precipice could take us to depression, to anger or to affection. They were all uncomfortable choices but I had to get to sentiment otherwise nothing made sense. I held my breath.

"Your grandparents stayed in one place and where did it get them? Nowhere, that's where. I'm showing you the world, broadening your horizons. Most children dream about having adventure. You don't have to dream, you live it."

The adventure speech. Janine was upbeat in this rendition as if we were headed for some exotic locale where a castle and loyal villagers awaited our arrival with bated breath. I looked out the window trying to gaze, to not listen, to not be in that old car bought for a song and a dance on that old road going to any old place for another odd job in a non-descript suburban development in a school with people who did not look like me and who spoke an odd language of boys and dances punctuated with *Tiger Beat* and Leif Garrett and scented with Watermelon Bonnie Bell. But gazing made my head hurt. The foreground moved too fast.

"Nothing ever stops, Darlene, even when it seems like everything is still it's not. The world is always turning, your blood is always moving. Things don't stop until you die and maybe not even then. There's a name for that. Somebody or another's theory or law or something. . . . Haven't you learned that in school yet?"

In that moment, I wasn't aware that I had learned anything in school. I tried not to cry, exhaled the knots in my chest and sipped on my barely cool 7-Up. *I hate this life.*

* * *

This time the road took us back to St. Louis to North Taylor and the Page Street Y. The birth town of both me and my mother. I didn't know the language there of the Saints Roller Rink, the Ville or the Triple A Donuts. It was a language from which I was kept away like a black hole, a wrinkle in time into which I might trip and fall, never to see a future. Where future—a fact on which I had come to rely, a word that represented my way out (or was it my way in)—was a foreign concept. The people there could live only in the here and now because there was only the here and now.

Granny's house was just five buildings and across the street from what was known as Grandma's corner, Sarah and West Belle Place, but when we got to my grandmother's house, I wasn't allowed to go beyond the garden in the backyard. I was to stay indoors with my mother's parents and two of her three surviving siblings and my mother when she cared to come out of her room. It was a family affair.

"You're going to be somebody, girl" Granny'd say while plaiting my hair.

* * *

"Jack and Jill? Let me tell you a little something about Jack and Jill." Uncle Sherm's voice always sounded as if he were about to have a coughing fit. His last coughing fit.

"Jack and Jill went up the hill to look down upon their brothers. College called, affirmative action for all, hard labor for the others. Paper bag tests, no civil unrest indoctrination for the masses." He laughed, coughed and laughed harder, amused with his self.

"Hush up, Sherman. Just cause your trifling ass couldn't go to college don't mean other people can't or shouldn't." My mother tapped her Kool on the edge of the pink glass ashtray and turned the page of the *Jet* magazine she had been reading aloud.

"I ain't saying she can't go." Uncle Sherm turned to me and took my hand. There was a dramatic deepening of his slouch now that his elbow was no longer propping him up on the kitchen table. He did not so much hold my hand as pull it down in an effort to hold his self up. His head was unsteady like a baby who's learning to balance the weight on a weak neck. I froze and focused on the Frosted Flakes box beyond his head. It seemed like he'd never let me go.

"Just don't get yourself indoctrinated. Just cause you can beat the bag with your pretty self don't mean you should take test." He winked and nodded simultaneously.

I looked to my grandmother then to my mother for some indication of what to do. Neither of them were paying any attention to me. I stepped back and felt my arm pulsate and cool where Uncle Sherm's warm damp hand had clutched it. He continued to laugh into the gold speckles in the kitchen table.

"Dumbass. They don't even do that shit anymore. You always trying to tell somebody something. Why don't you get your current events together and live in the present. Put down that *Night Train* or whatever mess it is you're into now." Janine, preparing to eat, covered her duck and noodles in a thick layer of red pepper. The powder melted into the brown sauce until was a gritty orange paste.

Uncle Sherm rambled on with stories about Black people being guinea pigs, the war, and the man. Janine said to pay him no mind, the shiffless so and so was always drunk and talking out the side of his neck. I had to listen though. His stories had life. They were not the smooth gray and beige stories of fishing trips, golf games, and Florida vacations I tuned out in the identical suburban apartment complexes I knew. There, people were leading preplanned lives in preplanned complexity with no tolerance for deviation. Here everything had been thrown out the window with the bathwater.

What was left was passion. Passionate anger. Passionate love. Passion gone awry. At first the lightening clap with which everything was done was threatening. I did not know that loquaciousness was a way of life, that volume meant "I love you" "you belong here." Here a quiet beige existence meant there was something wrong.

* * *

In time, I could hear everything that was happening around me and take it all in. It filled me and rolled around coursing in tides. I slept long and had intricate dreams with colors and rhythms that were new and rich. In waking hours I was finally allowed to play outside with the other children on the block as long as Granny was in the window watching.

I concentrated on turning a good double-dutch rope. Not letting it go clap. Not being distracted by the smooth brown skin laying itself over jumping muscles. Learning the cheers. Not focusing too hard on the lips and their thermotactic effect. The footsteps. Not letting my eyes rest too long near the hips. I rolled my neck and jumped in.

My name is Darla
Check
I am a Virgo
Check
I came to get down
Check
I got to get down
Check
So, Get on down get down get down get down
Woo!
So, Get on down get down get down get down.
Woo!

By the end of the fall Hank had found us. After a few days of groveling and apologizing, screaming and crying, we were on the road again. I had eased my way toward an internal kind of freedom.

Honey-baby-child, let me tell you. St. Louis was the second place I didn't want to leave.

Elissa G. Perry is a writer, performer and activist of African and Choctaw descent. She has published several stories, interviews and other writing in places such as *I Do I Don't, Black Silk, Beyond Definition, Clamour, Girlfriend Number One* and *Sinister Wisdom*.

Beto Palomar

I wandered one night into a poetry reading on the U.C. Berkeley campus. June Jordan and her students in Poetry for the People delivered a poetry that spoke plainly but beautifully with compelling rhythms and distinct imagery, in a way that, refreshingly, did not hide itself—did not mask itself in vague pretexts or pretensions of high abstracted art. That night I heard a clear poetry straight from people's hearts intended to communicate to members of a shared and beloved community. June really displayed to us the special place that poetry occupies, not only in the personal life of individuals, but as an essential cultural building block of cultures in the poetry of religious texts that consider the word to be sacred.

In my poetry, I try to write with purpose, with ultimate clarity of meaning in mind, whether through metaphor or imagery, seeking above all to communicate directly, always while enamored with the play of sounds of words across a line. My five years of teaching for the San Francisco WritersCorps (2003-2008) allowed me to share and test my writing against possibly the most fickle and difficult audience for poetry: the youth. Often I wrote with them in mind to win them over with examples of the day's lesson. Some of these poems continued to develop, and I let them take me to new places. Writing is sometimes a lonely act, but its meaning is not isolated. Poetry needs to live among us and talk to us, and WritersCorps gave me the chance to share those ideals with others, especially my own beloved community at International Studies Academy.

The Day the Mexicans Disappeared
after Guillermo Gómez-Peña

the day we disappeared
into some blackhole in space
(or maybe a brown-hole we don't know
much astrophysics)
many made sincere speeches about
how the problems of welfare, gangwars
and flatulence
vanished

into thin air
unaware
at that moment
350,000 white babies in wheelers
veered into streets
losing the guiding force
of caretaker Marias, Rosas, Carmelas
the white babies alone
pobrecitos
lost under Range Rovers
from Marin to Oklahoma City
what a pity
the day the mexicans disappeared
all the million dollar development
stopped
construction sites
more silent than libraries
the day the mexicans disappeared
trash piles reached the ceilings
of corporate offices
the managers could barely wade
through the corridors of cubicles
and the confetti
to reach their coffee breaks
there was no coffee
the day the mexicans disappeared
bean tree branches hung low to the ground
with no one to pick them
dry them, and carry to the market
on their backs in sacks like mules
the day the mexicans disappeared
grapes in the field lay swollen
bleeding wine back into the earth
intoxicating the worms and flies
the ripened strawberries melted
into mush as the grower landowners fumbled
pathetically stooping to pick
at least enough to keep the
bank foreclosure at bay
the army lost its soldiers
leaving the frontlines open

for whites to get shot down
the day the mexicans disappeared

Walter Whitman Nos Visit(o) un Domingo While Having Sacred Carne Asada

carne asada sizzles on the grill
the sacred life of a vaca donated, consecrated
we accept this carne,
dándonos vida
la comida
de una gallina,
o el rez
calm in the mexican
green
mexican
sweet
sustenance of carne
smoke wafting in the los angeles naked
fertile air of south central los
angeles
we los angeles, the angels of a brown
city savour life with a
carne asada cookout
gente, la familia invited
around the fire of the grill the
long carried pull of speaking round
the fire and speak
and tell jokes to provoke laughter
to erupt like so many ripe rains
water flowing from the agua de fresa fresca
agua de fresca red like lips
of my love's mouth
in comes the rude friend
Walter Whitman was his nombre
el vato Walter Whitman strolls
round our backyard entrada
smelling cada sabor of smoke
the onions crackling on the fiery metal
white bulbs crackling black

green burning, delicately crisp
attracts el gran poeta
Walter
he tells me
me dice que in his 48th manifestation
he lands Walter Whitman
de sur central
poeta, periodista
mexicano Walter
mexican como me
y cantaba sobre la lumbre feroz
controlada
fire in balance with the precision
of a propane valve
the lights white
electric star illumination
replaces fire but television never replaces
the will to tell stories
to sing of the electric
lights that light our life
in the south central night
cold and naked like me
Walter Whitman,
i told him that night
the song of the perro enjaulado
never fed the kibble
restricted neglected starving black dog
he howls the song of the black dog
in the nights the wretched howls
Walter Whitman, i told him of the song
of the helicopter blades
metal rhapsodic swirl slicing the
nights those
metal blades
pushing the air to fly
a song of chopper blades
piercing south central sky
Walter, chigando Walter, compadre,
where is the song, i ask him
of the sacred carne asada?
and he looks at me and says,

the song lies with
poets to come! orators, singers musicians to come!
I myself but write one or two indicative words for the future,
I but advance a moment only to wheel and hurry back into the darkness
leaving it to you to prove and define it
expecting the main things from you.
Walter me dice the songs
of sacred quemada carne asada
que la gente come on this sacred
black night
the songs of cebolla verde
como el color de vida
te doy a tí
lo encontraremos
con los poetas
of the carne asada nights

Beto Palomar is a Xicano poet and artist born and raised in Los Angeles and Watts. He is the author of the poetry collection *The Writing on the Walls*. He learned and taught poetry for the first time in June Jordan's Poetry for the People at U.C. Berkeley, where he graduated with a degree in interdisciplinary studies. He has taught poetry and art at colleges and high schools, including U.C.L.A. and International Studies Academy in San Francisco.

Aja Couchois Duncan

I had the opportunity to work with Writers-Corps in the late '90s. My primary teaching site was an emergency shelter for youth. The kids were that and sometimes older. They were all in crisis, and writing:

Dear Love,
I wonder about my heart; it shrinks every wilderness I see.

Some days their sorrow seemed too much for the room we occupied to bear. Some days there were no words at all. Other days, we wrote oral letters to the world.

I fear Sundays all day and evening . . . . When night comes to me
I feel disaster and my whole life seems translucent. I want to hold
on, but can't remember my address.

It was in writing through it that those young people taught me something I will carry always: sometimes the most we can do is to show up for ourselves, for one another. To hold time and attention and know that something better and worse is always on the other side.

Why does childhood make everything fearful and why is the sun
so far away? Love is something remorseful. I feel strange writing
things down because anyone can speak their blood to asphalt, be-
cause anyone hears you and sighs about time.

I will never forget the youth I met at the shelter, what they taught me about our collective capacity to live despite or perhaps because of. After we parted, I continued to teach language arts, leading writing workshops at universities, through college outreach programs, in juvenile hall. I wrote poetry with those who had been spoken to always of their brilliance and those who had been told only of their damage. The practice is the same; we all must find our own language for narrating self.

Some days, I follow the path that's hidden in my veins — every
time rain falls. I thank words for listening to me and no one will
say what tomorrow may believe — this isn't my other letter.

My own writing shifted as a result of teaching. I learned to let go of grammar, of the rigid order of syntactic sense. I became more interested in fictional non-fiction and hybrid genres that hover somewhere in between imagination and the contested field of history. It is here that our greatest possibility resides.

In Situ

i.

pluvial or pleistocene
fossilized cloak of night
masking population lush as willow
the shadowing, what we
alone   recover

land a narrow tongue nestled
against the sea, rivers swallowing

granite, silt, cyprus roots, her legs
thrust open, a passage among trout, kingfisher

antelope trails snaking the swollen flesh
her mouth opens to hermit thrush, swallow

exhale hawk and bear, the pink salmon
feed only when you are hungry

talk of stubborn children tossed to sky
outline the shape of dusk and wait

they will speak of you always
wretched diggers

ii. seriation

a method of dating
kitchen ware, weaponry, human hair
relative to wind, pollen
drought or slaughter
how they explain so much damage
as if two worlds, empty and full
moving in-between

snow dusts the canyon its seasons of church, people
flushed west as cow replaces buffalo, timid sheep
hunting each other or waiting for the truckloads of men
snow mobiles and shotguns blasting this shape of america,
a study of horse meat and syphilis

wind as white river or charcoal smudged across the page
of trees darkened by ants moving along the nude bark
as small colonies or herds of cattle bend their heads
towards grass buried by snow knowing what lies beneath
but waiting as she waits for him to return or to die beneath
the blanket erasing his shrunken body moving
from one white field to another explosion of snow
the force of desire its nucleus

iii. evidence

a) Lake Ines and Alba
  two sisters who drowned
  in the spring the forest
  mourned mountain lions
  tearing at the cold flesh
  raw scar of wood

b) four point buck shot
  with obsidian two inches
  from thunder, the coyotes survived
  all winter their young nibble the strips
  of meat torn like bacon from the deer's
  hind legs, clumps of hair
  blood, drained free

c) empty school yard children locked inside tucked behind
  desks their toes tapping the wood floor he writes help
  with the point of his shoe while the teacher reviews
  the vocabulary words he misspelled manipulate but
  his ears are their own language of punishment
  small and malformed as brussel sprouts the green wounds

iv. archeology

a science of waste and wonder
she weaves baskets of redbud and willow
stitching coils, human intestines

nocharo mu

       don't touch me

made human by franciscans mapping nudity in wool
her newborn daughter twisting the umbilical cord
running her soundless cries her breast so full of milk she
has to stop and bleed her wings drowning her husband
still bent knees in the chapel mouth tacky with barley
soundless prayers his wife in hell the priest tells him
not walking the trail from field to church mourning infant
of one breath even if he feels her next to him at night bound
to the bed the last three months of pregnancy more restless
than before only hours free to birth a world she must bury
her fist collapsing landslide

3 wool blankets
3 axes
3 hoes
some clothing
glass beads

       antelope   the bowels or entrails
          a severed tongue
         legs

          dangling snow

v. chronology

another layer of habitation
another back to replace your slip
beneath the weight of

> *fu-sang*
> lip of the pacific
> silk and brine

sampans rode the black tide
culled abalone   iridescent ears of the sea
could not hear grandmother yee
sing or chong   their erasure
from the record so simple really
to remove the yellow stain

whose name do you carry the sloped shoulders of a father
his back crisp beneath the sun almost purple as a beet
his arm still toils inside of you second cousin to another
paper person who harvests sugar from soil attempt
strange fricatives with your tongue and remember
he chose this place california is gold mountain this land
its breast and valleys a ghost moaning its limbs
breaking apart

an owls cries dusk moon mirrors asphalt as if river
a fawn grazes the golf course hungers to test her new found
strength she pauses near the stop sign oblivious to its hue
must cross between cars maintain an even speed the night
a truck turns two wheels airborne one hand in his hair
his wife itching the pale scalp the fawn has four legs
to contend with two more than she imagines match
her stride count them off to yourself her mother taught her
rhythm motions her siblings so quick the fawn still
straddling the bank and singing night one two bounding
across the street one leg bends back she falters three
her head turns away from the truck as if only a bird
chasing ground her eyes capturing the winged light

vi. soil

burden a rock or the knocking train its roar of moon
and stumble no animal can imitate its reach or bind
the miles of tracks their trust in rows a sick engine runs
its own language across mountains the stitched earth
claims those *wretched heathens*

but not the ones who now traverse land as if history
swept clean as if landscape provided its own erasure
or death smoothed the rough tracks

and echo this diction such an ugly language sound
when darkness is made memory and geology
an unnatural burial

ghosts will not remain in situ they hover and spit
cover your head keep running hide in the relentless
motion of day

Aja Couchois Duncan's writing has been anthologized in *Biting the Error: Writers Explore Narrative* (Coach House Press), *Bay Poetics* (Faux Press) and *Love Shook My Heart 2* (Alyson Press). An educator of Ojibwe, French and Scottish descent, she holds an M.F.A. in creative writing from San Francisco State University.

Monica A. Hand

I am reminded of when I first found Poetry. I was ten. Suddenly I could talk back to the adults around me, make commentary on what I thought was wrong with things, play with my dreams, and even be someone else if I wanted to. I could be like Langston Hughes and Audre Lorde: self-determined. I could cry, laugh, mourn, dance about, lie around, scorn and contemplate, justify and belly crawl. Defy death.

WritersCorps was my open door, new air at a time when I was struggling to breathe, to pay the rent, and otherwise provide for my two children. No doubt, it was an income, a chance to make a living—but a chance to make a living doing something that I loved.

WritersCorps became a way for me to make a difference, a way to give back what had been given to me—a love for language, words, diction, story. The miracle of the program is that you're not just teaching language skills, you're building self-esteem and society. I was an artist doing the work of the people. I was a soldier passing on an essential survival skill, the art of metaphor, the art of shape shifting.

Me and Romare at the Depot

Going train, going train, whistling
Choking locomotive like the rooster's crow
We all dressed up in our Sunday best
No where to go, no where to go

Steaming train, a genie's three wishes
This ain't my body, just my face, my frown
Got something ancient on my mind
There's a fair-skinned boy at the depot

He and I, we got somewhere to go
Traveling train, you're like the guitar man
Dust off your hat, and shine your shoes
Tap the rhythm, gotta go

Far away from this here town
Going train, going train, whistling

Talisman

Nellie Mae with red and blue ink
draws sacred lines, shapes that heal
bird collages braced against evil
With perched claws and hands that speak

her colored pencils are magic wands
With things lost, she unleashes
howling dogs thirsty for justice
if our children are met with harm

Inside her felt tip marker—faith
Her paper dresses seal out pain
Crayon parachutes keep spirits safe
flies them far away from these here times

to a happy place where nobody hurts children
to a happy place where nobody hurts children

Bound

Me and Rosadel, we are in Upward Bound at Seton Hall, a summer program just for us city kids who are college bound. English, Math, History, Science. But it's mostly about us. Black people. Not Negroes; Black People. Our teachers are college students home from school for the summer. They talk about Revolution, about change. And they are proud. They are Black and they are proud. They teach us how to move our feet. We journalize, write poetry; draw and film our neighborhoods, stage Lorraine Hansberry's *To Be Young Gifted and Black*. Each flat nose girl is Nina Simone, singing from her gut—angry, then sad, then proud. They say it is the new Black National Anthem. Me and Rosadel, we are college bound, upward bound. I write a poem about living in the projects even though I really live in a three-family house on Ninth Avenue. Rosadel makes a pretty dashiki from a Vogue pattern. We are young, gifted and Black. And we are proud.

Monica A. Hand founded and directed the Poetry Slam Academy, modeled after her experiences with D.C. WritersCorps. Her poetry can be found in *Beyond the Frontier: African American Poetry for the 21st Century* and *Seven Seasons*.

D. Scot Miller

I'm from a working-class town in West Virginia. It may sound dramatic, but my best friends are either dead or in jail, and if I had not received a letter from WritersCorps inviting me to California, I might be with those friends now. Riding the California Zephyr with Chris West, landing in the fog-covered city with him—it was more than a turning point, it was a jumping-off. I have a son here, I have published here, taught here, and I have loved and loved and loved. San Francisco is more than my home, it is my heart. I was young, brash, and full of myself, so my bluster often drowned out my gratitude, but WritersCorps gave me a chance to live a life of my dreams.

In WritersCorps, I was introduced to San Francisco as an artist, writer and teacher. The first people I met and loved here were similarly engaged—relationships which have endured and proven to be meaningful in ever-increasing ways. WritersCorps gave me chutzpah, or should I say huevos?—as a testing ground for my youthful talent and drive. Often, I would find myself among gifted people who were taking the time to consider my work. I would be praised, and I would be shamed. I would be called to the mat and placed in the spotlight. Though I'd been published in a few places, it was the other Writers-Corps teachers of that first year that gave me apotheosis. I was no longer a writer and teacher because I said so, but because it was my profession and craft.

As a writer, I believe in the process more than the product. I write something every day: a poem, an essay, a love letter, a thesis, a press release. I believe there is no writing without social engagement—without interacting with all different kinds of people from different walks of life. I tell stories, sing songs, scratch on walls, the sum and total of all I've experienced and of all the people I've met. My soul, my well-being, my contribution, my solace, my pain—everything brings me back to the page. I used to describe this affliction as "carto-mania," but as I've pulled together my body of work, I have settled on describing my writing as Afro-Surrealistic Expressionism, in the tradition of Henry Dumas. I write from the absurd conditions of my personal, political, artistic experience and historical placement.

Post-Apocalyptic Blues

The night before
with my family 'round
To get my rest
I laid me down
To get my rest
I laid me down

I dreamed a dream so real to me
That I knew twern't nothing shorta prophesy
Nothing short of prophesy

I seen the sky open up and them riders on the wing
I seen the sky bust wide open from them riders on the wing
The people was locked inside theyselves
So ordered by the king

And the king he was an ignorant man
From his house up on the hill
The king had not stepped one tender foot
From his house up on the hill
He left the dead to tend the dead
He loosed the killers to kill
He left the dead to tend the dead
and loosed the killers to kill
(Talkin' 'bout Cheney and his boys, dogs of war, yeah)

All the buildings was still standing
But wasn't no one inside
All the buildings was still standing
But wasn't no one inside
Like them folks all disappeared
When wasn't no place left to hide
No place left to hide

I woke to the sound of thunder
like the beginning of the end
I woke alone to the sound of thunder
and the howl of a lonely wind
Each and every member of my family
I never saw again.

Revisited

Far flung black one
Longside of five broke down boroughs
Stepped and fetched 'long six ivory towers
Slipped and I staggered through countless dead barrooms
Screamed out in front of 13 deaf judges
Scattered through space in sorrow

A new sprung seed whose leaves were all crippled
An ocean of diamonds in a sea of black blood
Gold pyramids wit eyes full of laughter
A set of dice that always rolled snake-eyes
A bank vault with a cracked glass ceiling
Million profits in brown suits in lead boxes

Sirens singing like the first birds of morning
Man-made thunder clap that whipped the world
A million kindred shake ten million shackles
Half a million marching and nobody lookin'
Ten people starve and one person laughing
The song of a poet getting showered with bullets
The sound of the teacher as she cried at the market

Long strugglin' dun going back out to streets
Walk that dark mile to the sea
Build a hush harbor and use it as haven
Plant your own garden and grow your own trees
The fires first burn from the day we awaken
When the time so long promised has finally come

Tell it, Speak it, and Think it, and breathe it
and resound from the soundbox so we all can hear it
Spit it and shout it until you know how it happened
Make them cut you down before you stop rappin'

D. Scot Miller is a San Francisco Bay Area writer, visual artist, curator and teacher. Author of the poetry collection *Slicker* and the Afro-surreal *Knot Frum Hear*, he is a regular contributor to the *East Bay Express*, *SF Weekly*, *YRB NYC*, *Popmatters* and *Showcase Magazine*. He is a founder of The Black Bard Writing Collective and serves on the board of *Nocturnes (Re)view*.

Dirty & Alive We Cried

Danielle (Dani) Montgomery

I think writing is a way of life. I've been writing poetry since I was about sixteen. My poetry explores themes of class, queer sexuality and mental illness and celebrates the beauty of survival under difficult circumstances. It makes connections between our personal experiences and the need for radical social change. Through the everyday details, my writing aims to show us our extraordinary potential.

WritersCorps was an opportunity for me to learn more about this extraordinary potential. At the Center for Young Women's Development, I met young women who were brilliant and resourceful. Together we used words to challenge the wrongs we saw around us: racism, sexism, poverty, homophobia. I was privileged to "teach" these young women and to be a part of a truly revolutionary organization.

Now that I am a mother, I have a new perspective on WritersCorps. As I witness my children developing language skills, from the first gurgles to the first words to the first sentences, I am struck again by how important language is. The power of language to name, to bless, to condemn, to illuminate, is not to be underestimated. WritersCorps shares this power with young people who may be thinking it's not theirs to own. And it is. It is all of ours.

december seventh

seven months pregnant
my mother smoked a pack of cigarettes
drank a pot of coffee
and scrubbed the floor on hands and knees

that night it stormed hard
i slid out early
cold and blue
umbilical cord tied around my neck
smelling like soap and smoke and coffee grounds

she cradled me in one hand
under fluorescent hospital lights
sucking sterile air we cried
dirty and alive

hot check days

after we spent her paycheck
and rolled all the pennies
after we spent every last dime
we could find hiding in drawers
under the couch cushions or in old coat pockets
after no check came from grandma
and we'd eaten the last packet of ramen
with the last stale saltines
mom would smile
like this was a holiday
she'd load us into her aging navy blue oldsmobile
drive to the biggest grocery store in town
and tell us *pick anything*
we'd streak up and down aisles
grabbing whatever we could carry
soda and chewy granola bars
individually wrapped snak paks of chips
every last flavor of kool aid
boxes of fish sticks and apple jacks
hungry man salisbury steaks
with super sized mashed potatoes
we'd hurl it all into her basket
wondering
how we could run out of the store
with so much stuff
but while we stood close to each other and watched
our mother pushed the cart up to the counter
chatted with the cashier
and wrote a check for forty dollars over—
he even said *thank you ma'am*
as he handed it to her—
she grinned back *no, really, thank YOU*
and wheeled us into the parking lot
well, now we have gas money
she'd say
who wants to see a movie?

tucson

arizona summer
cooks like an oven
that nobody can turn off
the air so thick with heat
it puddles up in ditches
shimmers like water
the smell of fire hangs heavy
everything red   burning
all of creation stays still and listens
to the chorus of rattlesnakes and cicadas
the buzz of mosquitoes

i would sit on the swing
stir up dustclouds with my toes
stare at the sun till its shape burned into my eyes
thinking death must be like the summer sky
empty yet heavy
or lie under the carport
sucking a popsicle
and daydream monsoons
flash floods and thunderstorms

on fridays after dinner
dad would drive us to dairy queen
in his sky blue station wagon
with the plastic seats that burned
diamonds into the backs of my legs
he'd buy a butter scotch cone for mom
a chocolate one for me and
the three of us would sit on splintery benches
under the sagging patio with
christmas lights still dripping from it
dad talking about how things were looking up
and we could pay off the bills soon
mom pretending to believe and me
sitting in the middle just smiling as the sun set.

sometimes a storm would roll in
at night you wouldn't notice

till rain started dropping on the tin roof
a sound like nails thrown into a bucket
we would run out into the dirt lot
let the rain seep into our skin
slide over our faces into our open mouths
all crazy with laughing
as if rain was gold and we
were about to be rich
no more dust and sweat
and waiting.

Danielle (Dani) Montgomery is a queer poet living in the San Francisco Bay Area. The mother of two girls, she holds an M.F.A. from Mills College, and her work has appeared in *Molotov Mouths: Explosive New Writing* (Manic D Press), *The Civil Disobediance Handbook* (Manic D Press), and numerous journals, chapbooks and zines.

marcos ramírez

© marcos ramírez

There we were in the first year of WritersCorps, this motley gathering of 24 or so writers, all there for the love of writing and teaching—all there in disbelief that we were getting paid to teach creative writing, by a whole program devoted to writing and supported by the government! In all, the experience cemented my belief in a thoroughly democratic education—an education not dependent on rote memorization, but an invigorating, engaging, respectful and rigorous curriculum that involved student participation at every turn. Yes, I did it for $5.15 an hour, but that never bothered me. What bothered me was that writing—poetry, fiction, drama—was not respected or encouraged in the school environment. The writing arts were seen as peripheral or elective or all-together useless in comparison to the almighty and increasingly bland expository essay. My students were told by their teachers to stop writing about their lives in creative fashions, and instead to write formally about historical figures that alienated them from their own education. Or worse yet, they were told to fastidiously learn a trade. I was enraged by this judgment placed on creative writing and even more so by the immediate tracking of my students into trade professions.

As a youth living in poverty, only a few years earlier, I was treated the same way, ushered toward trade schools and community colleges, despite my strong grades. Now, as an educator, I wanted it to be better for my students. I felt that they were being steered away from the beauty of poetry, the illumination of fiction and the immediacy of plays—and in the same gesture they were being steered away from their own lives—into thinking of themselves and their voices as peripheral. I never see my job as writer or teacher as one that involves speaking for my "voiceless" students. On the contrary, I see my job as ensuring that my students employ the voices they have had all along, employ them with stinging clarity and with the most evocative and provocative words they can put together. To compel a listener, or a reader—to demand from them their full attention with just the felicity and lucidity of words. That is in no way peripheral, but entirely central to the education of my students. Working with WritersCorps supported me in maintaining not only the life of an artist and teacher, but in my everyday comings and goings on this beloved earth.

ode to la tortilla

mi abuelita's hands
scoop you out of moist maza
like god scoops clay to sculpt adam
she molds you in her holy hands
shapes you in her image
no not flat
but round and balanced
as you take the smacks and claps of life into you
in a rapid movement of ritual
her palms your first womb
her thumbs your first heartbeat
you lay onto her comal
where you harvest heat
know the meaning of creation
how humidity births your edible
flesh
you turn over with a whisk of her wrist
heat peppers your entire body
with brown delicious birthmarks
n with your edge crisp n ready
you glide your way
onto our dinner table
where your brothers n sisters wait for you
safe n snug
incubating underneath
a bed of steamy towels
fogging up the kitchen windows
condensing evidence
for all the neighborhood to know
everyday you sit at the head of mi familia's table
swing en mi papá's hands
swim en mi hermano's menudo
pinwheel onto mi mamá's frijoles
for hundreds n hundreds of years
through conquest and genocide
through revolution n earthquakes
you the eucharist
from my ancestor's hands
who kisses our hungry lips

marbles

i pick up a stick
then kick some rocks
with my nine year old feet
n find five marbles just sittin there
on the dirt road
small little treasures de guatemala
i got two coca-colas
two pan dulces
n some chiclets for the walk back

i head towards el campo
where all the war orphans live
to play fútbol
with my new best friend mario
the cute one with the pretty eyes
who tells me to give it my all
when i butt the ball with my head

as i reach el campo
i see his back first
mario's body
danglin
on a wooden cross
n i mumble to myself
between my trembles
los soldados
los soldados

as i walk towards la policía
i see mario's head near the goal post
no shock just numbness inside of me
his face starin up at me
dirty n bloody
flies n ants crawling in n out of his eye sockets
they hacked it off with a machete
then kicked it to try to make a goal
i know it
i know it

la policía find a bunch of eyes

inside a circle in the dirt
los soldados play marbles with them
when they get bored
they're just kids themselves
la policía say to one another

i don't know what to do
but my gut tells me to pray
n as i kneel before mario's head
i reach out to it
my hands shakin
like mi abuelita's wrinkled hands
when she knits
place two of the marbles
i found on the road
into mario's eye sockets

the shiny green ones
pretty
just like mario's

marcos ramírez has taught at June Jordan's Poetry for the People for fifteen years where he currently serves as the program coordinator. He was born in Richmond, California, and lives in San Francisco's Tenderloin District.

© Angela Lang

Alison Seevak

As a narrative poet, I have always been interested in the way poetry allows me to distill experience and make sense of my life and the world around me. Years ago, before I taught for the San Franciso WritersCorps, I had a student who put into words what I believe as both writer and teacher. Hanh Le was a fifth grader who'd recently exchanged the water buffalo and rice fields of her Vietnamese village for the broken glass and concrete sidewalks of West Oakland. "My life is not a blank piece of paper," Hanh wrote in English, a language she was just beginning to learn. It's been almost fifteen years, but Hanh's words have stayed with me. No one's life is a sheet of blank paper. My goal as a teaching artist is to nurture in my students the belief that their experience is worth getting down on the page, along with helping them develop the tools to do so.

I taught for WritersCorps for three powerful and profound years, from 1998 to 2001. I led writing groups for kids at Mercy Housing (a nonprofit housing development) and for new immigrants at Newcomer High School, and was the teaching writer in a collaborative visual arts and literary project at a community arts center. Sometimes my students turned somersaults under their desks, or during a lesson on metaphor compared my teeth to yellow corn kernels. But mostly, they blew me away with their words. Like Hanh, many of them had left one country for another and were learning two new languages—English and poetry. Or they were the children of immigrants bearing the responsibility of being the bridge between two worlds.

Beyond WritersCorps, I've continued to lead writing workshops in public schools and a library near my home in Albany, California. My current students lead lives more comfortable and privileged than the WritersCorps youth I knew. But my years with WritersCorps confirmed and strengthened my belief that poetry can make a difference— whether it is to the boy from China searching for a way to grieve the best friend left behind in Guangzhou or the sullen suburban kid diagnosed with a litany of learning disabilities. His classroom teacher tells you that he can barely write a sentence, but when he finally turns over a ragged ball of paper, you find a perfect, startling simile, a shining star he'd crumpled in his fist.

Women's Shelter, Butte, Montana

No one had ever hit me.
But I was new in town
and a friend's friend said
the place would be empty,
I could stay there.
I was asleep the night
the girl and her mother
came in off the reservation.
Everything they owned
in two black garbage bags
they dragged across the highway,
because they were broke
and scared and moving fast.
I didn't hear any of it,
wasn't even supposed to be
there, amidst the bunk beds,
dusty cereal boxes,
and romance novels, I had
a brand-new college diploma
and my father's credit card
so I could call home
Sunday nights.
I only knew enough to know
that I knew nothing.
But I was learning.
The woman in sunglasses
pouring Cheerios in the kitchen.
The way the girl woke me
that first morning,
practicing steps for a pow wow
dance, small feet beating
a tattoo on linoleum.
Every morning,
that pounding, a warning.
I hadn't met you yet.
Hadn't laid my head against
your chest, tasted your salt
on my tongue.
Hadn't spent the afternoons

in the wooden bed
your wife's grandfather carved.
I only knew enough to know
that I knew nothing. Not even
as much as the girl when
I took her out for breakfast.
She had never seen
the inside of a restaurant.
When the waitress brought us
cold water in tall glasses
she asked *Do we have to pay for it?*
I shook my head. *No, it was free.*
She already knew nothing else was.

Lei Lei

Piece of jade on red thread
around her sweet neck,
she won't take it off,
her mother says. They gave
it to her at the orphanage
with her name—
Lei Lei, Gentle.
It's Memorial Day
in a friend's backyard,
grill going, yellow stars burst
on tomato plants.
I think the kids pump
too high on the swings,
but what do I know?
I'm not a mother. Yet,
they let me join their circle
on the grass, talk of schools
and pediatricians, why there aren't
advice nurses anymore.
Lei Lei doesn't want
her Chinese face, her mother sighs,
says she wants an English one,
like me.

I eye the flying kids,
ask, Don't you worry
the swings will tip?
Nah, the mothers swagger.
One's son had scabs
on his chin his first three years.
She says grave injury or death,
that's what scares me.
Lei Lei on the rickety slide
calls look, look, before
she dives. Her mother
jumps, then holds back
as if she can't protect her
from anything.

Alison Seevak has over ten years of experience teaching creative writing to youth in public schools, libraries and after-school programs. Her poetry and essays have appeared in *The Sun, Atlanta Review, Many Mountains Moving*, the *San Francisco Chronicle Book Review* and elsewhere. She holds a B.A. from Duke University, an M.P.H. from U.C. Berkeley and an M.F.A. in poetry from Vermont College. She lives in Albany, California with her daughter, Anna.

© Craig Hayes

Michele Kotler

My sixth-grade teacher inspired me to begin writing as a way to voice what I wanted to change, what I needed to release so as not to explode. He called me *poet*. I work to honor that title in my writing and in my teaching. I write to braid the influences of time and circumstance, mirroring the ways in which identity is shaped by its environment. Rhythm is a constant source of inspiration and structure. I believe poems are bridges.

WritersCorps was a bridge in a similar way. Working with Bronx youth, teens, parents, seniors and domestic violence survivors at New Settlement Apartments, I learned that a writing workshop is an important community organizing tool. I also learned that I had to grow as a writer if I wanted to grow new writers. I relearned the power of voice as I witnessed how we together could be listened to and have our aspirations and concerns taken seriously. We felt less frustrated. We felt the possibility of change. I remember one girl in particular who had just lost her mother to AIDS. Her feelings were locked down and it was difficult for anyone to reach her. After much prodding she wrote for me, and it was the first time she had "spoken" about the loss. It gave me and her community a way in, and it allowed her to begin the challenging work of opening up to something painful but necessary. She kept coming back to the workshop to write out what she couldn't yet say out loud.

I would go on to found an organization based on my WritersCorps experiences, and the work continues to be as critical as it is rewarding. My commitment to social engagement continues to define me as a writer.

Two poems from *Out of Order*

a poetry novella about doing time with an incarcerated loved one

Dance Card From Rikers, Downstate & Ogdensberg Correctional

I shared the floor with your first Love, the surprise on your face, never seen your eyes open quite that wide when we both, unplanned, showed up, me first, her an hour later, we laughed all day at your expense, and how expensive it was to be with you was something we talked about later as we drank our way into an upstate night and talked far too much about how much we knew it would never be the same   shared the floor with your father mother and brother never played so hard a card game learned it was easier if I lost because feeling lucky inside felt the opposite of winning

shared the floor with Wolf (the only man you said you fought inside) his lady Natalie later gave me a ride home it was clear Wolf hadn't told her made me think what you didn't tell me

shared the floor with a man who saved your life, can't remember his name but his woman's name *Gloria Gloria* looked like she knew this inside inside out   shared the floor with a grandma who kept getting warnings from the guards because she was slapping her grandson's face so hard you could hear it half way across the room

shared the floor with a guard that really liked you this guard would make it a point to squeeze your shoulder to let you know we had five more minutes   shared the floor with a man who in seven hours entertained three different women and I can't even remember how many children how he master-timed it so no woman saw the other was a dance in itself

shared the floor with a man whose state issued glasses were from the '70s he had been in that long and still his mother bent like something half broke was there dancing with us all shared the floor with a little girl who just walked up to you put her arms out so you could pick her up onto your lap this was illegal a guard grabbed her hand and pulled her away and she didn't cry but just kept looking back as if she needed to see you

when I left the floor that day that little girl who was maybe four years old stayed with me how did she know how to dance and not cry how long had it taken her to learn how long would it take her to forget?

We Have Jokes

we joke
how it could be lonely
even a little uneven
going from
being one
in 2,000,000
held tight
by a system
to one in
600,000
released
as in paroled
as in roll over
and beg or don't beg
and see what happens

we joke at how even the zeros
who never thought
they would be considered
don't know where to go

we joke that for now you are free not to worry
about what to do after being freed
by an industry that is thriving
and giving small towns the boost
of a life   time

we joke
at how our conversations are recorded
and that is why we insist on such quality
from each other

isn't it nice to know
that each thirty minute call
isn't being used for training purposes
that the recording is just the government
protecting me or even you
from what we can't imagine

you try to laugh at how
MCI calls asking me to join *our neighborhood plan*
I ask them if they know
that their neighborhood is a network of so many prisons
they should offer a new kind of collective calling
sign up for five years and you will get a free calendar
that doesn't stop at December

you make me laugh at how the Correction Officer at 7 AM count
hates the number thirty-
one   twenty-three   or forty-seven
hates any digit that he can't make it past
as he tries to count you
today it was eighteen that screwed him up
we joke that his wife is a math teacher
who loves him for the numerals
on his prison paycheck

we joke that at the end of your sentence
we will receive an offer in the mail
all your recorded conversations
dated and playable
yours for only $79.56
the cost of a single day of incarceration
in a non leap year

we joke at how when made to wait
for upstate visit hours to begin
I helped a correction officer pen a haiku
to his lady friend   convinced him that
if a 2nd grader can do it so can he
convinced him to use love as one
of his syllables and while I was
three hours deep
into the visit with you
he came over and thanked me
and you laughed at how
this was the Correction Officer who had trouble counting
and we laughed that maybe syllables were easier
to add up than grown men

we joke
at how when you first came in
you looked older
more tired
and now
you look younger than the new upstatees
as if this place agreed with you
as if anyone could agree
with this place

Michele Kotler is the founding director of the Community-Word Project, an arts-in-education organization based in New York City. She holds an M.F.A. in poetry from the University of Michigan and a B.A. from Sarah Lawrence College. She performs her poetry in New York City and her work has appeared in journals such as *Washington Square* and *Painted Bride Quarterly*.

Gamal Abdel Chasten

The written words of writers are the stories of their experience and heart bled onto canvas. Those stories grow, the words become more expressive as the writer continues to experience life. In my house growing up, music and art were practiced and encouraged. The Signifying Monkey, Richard Pryor, Nikki Giovanni, Muhammad Ali, country, jazz and soul are some of the textures that influenced me as an artist.

I grew from the pen to the open mic and ultimately to the theater, telling stories as a songwriter/poet, playwright and then screenwriter. I began working for WritersCorps at a pivotal point in my career, in making the transition to full-time artist. I had found my artistic voice and I had a responsibility to help others find theirs.

Working at Nelson Avenue Family Residence, a tier two shelter, and many other sites in the Bronx, I became a tool that aided young people in discovering their love and talent for the written word. There is nothing more valuable than teaching to help you learn more about what it is you are trying to teach. One thing I learned is that every stage of your life is essential in shaping your voice. Thank you, WritersCorps.

From the play *The Last Word*

The Funeral Procession

(House fades to black. Lights fade up. The procession, upstage center in silhouette, is both a funeral and a jazz procession at the same time. The Ringmaster [procession leader] is seated downstage off-center stage. The Ringmaster represents he who guides us from this life to our next. The Ringmaster delivers his opening monologue to the audience introducing the cast of characters.)

RINGMASTER:
It was 1971, or was it 1917?
I was full-grown or maybe knee high
When I saw my first death march
A Jazz funeral go by.
Come to think

It might have been a circus come to town
Spilling down the street like bourbon
People frowning upside down.
French quarter dimes
Singing joyous sad songs
Crooked straight lines
Past a street named boulevard.
Wives swappin today
For the past 30 years
Husbands above ground
Buried but still here.
Back then, right now
I forget that I remember.
It was January, April
May or maybe December
I ain't quite certain, but this here is for sure
Ask my poppa or my Ma what everyone was so happy for
And she say, he say somebody left behind
A heap a trouble for somebody else to find.

(Lights fade. Ringmaster exits stage left.)

Scene One

(Lights up on John and his mother, Olivia, two of three surviving members of the Hancock family. They stand downstage right.)

JOHN:
So Poppa got his plot already.

MOTHER:
That's right we got them at Crossroads Cemetery a few years ago, they had a two for one sale.

JOHN:
Then that means everything is taken care of, the funeral, the flowers . . .

MOTHER:
Oh the flowers! I got a huge bouquet of plastic flowers.

JOHN:
Plastic flowers?

MOTHER:
They were dirt-cheap.

JOHN:
What am I doing here, so many days before the funeral?

MOTHER:
What do you mean?

JOHN:
Poppa is dead?

MOTHER:
Yes, of course.

JOHN:
You handled everything all by yourself?

MOTHER:
That's right.

JOHN:
So what could you possibly need me for?

MOTHER:
To grieve.

JOHN:
To grieve?

MOTHER:
That's right.

JOHN:
Why would you need me for that?

MOTHER:
I just thought it would be nice for you, your sister, and I to do some crying together.

JOHN:
Crying, isn't that just a little bit depressing?

MOTHER:
I don't understand.

JOHN:
The crying is bad enough, but then there's the hearse, the pre-show . . .

MOTHER:
Pre-show? I don't understand.

JOHN:
Yeah, that thing where they show the body.

MOTHER:
It's called a *wake*. *(Comedic drum role.)*

JOHN:
Well then there's the dirt, all that godforsaken dirt. I'm talking about my $40 dollar patent leather shoes in the dirt.

MOTHER:
Your father always said he wanted to be buried face down, so that way when people came to pay their last respects, they'd be able to kiss his ass goodbye.

(Lights fade out.)

• •

Final Curtain
(Light up on John and Jacqueline Hancock [brother and sister]. They are seated at a funeral parlor in preparation of their father's burial. They are in discussion with the assistant funeral director who is a bit OCD.)

ASSISTANT FUNERAL DIRECTOR:
So the final viewing of the body will take place at 6:45 AM for those who could not make it yesterday. One hour later there will be a group of morbid looking mourners wearing dark colored clothing knocking at your door, and they'll be saying things like, my condolences, and how are the children holding up, things like that. Now the proper response for you as the family would be as follows: it would have pleased him to know you were here. You need to repeat after me, I am doing this for your benefit. Again! It would have pleased him

FAMILY:
It would have pleased him

AFD:
To know you were here, and thank you so much

FAMILY:
To know you were here

AFD:
Thank you so much

FAMILY:
Thank you so much

AFD:
For visiting him in the hospital

FAMILY:
For visiting him in the hospital

AFD:
Correct, that's perfect. Now once everyone is ready, those in the most visible, emotional pain will be leading the pack. Oh, and we hired some extras, some state troopers to block off the road, and some soldiers from the armed services . . .

JOHN:
Poppa couldn't stand the army.

AFD:
Now we know your father wasn't patriotic but during this sensitive time our country is going through, it can only add to the moment, only add.

Once we reach the church you would have cried approximately three times. Now don't get out of the car on your own, it'll make you look too strong, too in control. Let the driver open up the car door, and then proceed directly to the church rec room. If you don't know how to find it, stop right where you are.

Now do you have dark sunglasses?

• •

Scene Five: Reading of the Will
(Lights up. The Hancock family — Olivia, Jonathon and Jacqueline — gathered at home for the reading of the will.)

LAWYER:
Ok, before we get started I need to ask if everyone who is mentioned in the will is present?

JOHN:
Why don't you take a roll call or something?

LAWYER:
If you think that's necessary, maybe that's not such a bad idea. The children listed are, Jacqueline Hancock, and John Hancock. In case you were not to survive him everything would be left to your mother and Ms. Ida Levy.

MOTHER:
Ida Levy! Who the hell is Ida Levy?

LAWYER:
Obviously someone your husband cared enough about to mention in his will.

JOHN:
This should be really interesting.

JACQUELINE:
Will you stop?

JOHN:
I'm just saying.

LAWYER:
Is there a problem here?

MOTHER:
Yes, there's a problem some strange woman is listed in this will . . .

JACQUELINE:
Mama . . .

MOTHER:
That's got to be a mistake.

JACQUELINE:
Mama . . .

MOTHER:
We are Hancocks, not Levys.

JACQUELINE:
Mama, isn't Ida Levy the woman you used to baby sit for when I was . . .

MOTHER:
What's that got to do with her mentioned in his fucking will!

LAWYER:
If it's okay with you, Mrs. Hancock, I should probably continue. And I should also mention that parts of this will may seem a little unorthodox.

MOTHER:
Really! I can't believe this, now he's gonna fuck me over from the grave.

JACQUELINE:
Don't let it get to you, just breathe through it.

MOTHER:
Breathe through it, you sound as stupid as your brother. I don't know anyone who has been fucked as much as I have, without having a hand put on 'em. But I think your brother was right when he said we should communicate. So listen while I communicate this: This is *my time*, my moment, and now I'm sitting at the *head* of the table. Here is where my life begins. So here's a toast. To me, Poppa's gone, and I've arrived. Now let this beautiful man finish his job.

LAWYER:
Um, thank you Mrs. Han—

MOTHER:
That's Ms . . . Ms Dupree. Dupree is my maiden name. You can call me by my maiden name Ms. Dupree.

Gamal Abdel Chasten has worked with the poetry and theater ensemble Universes for the past twelve years, in writing and developing two off-Broadway shows, The Ride and Slanguage. He was featured on HBO's Def Poetry Jam, and his individual projects include the plays God Took Away His Poem and The Last Word, and the screenplays Red Moon and Joe Bloe. His directing credits include The Last Word and Full Circle's Innerviews at Dance Theater Workshops.

© Alexis Vabre

Chrissy Anderson-Zavala

I grew up on the outskirts of Salinas, California, surrounded by the history of Cesar Chavez and Dolores Huerta, the stories of my family working in the strawberry fields, and the novels of John Steinbeck. In an agricultural community like this one, distance and silence pervade one's life, from whom you are allowed to love to the passive acceptance of many youths' particular brilliance lost in our deficient education system. Writing has always been a way for me to face and name that which feels too big and daunting to confront, a way to cope with the silences in a society that does not value youth voices.

In June Jordan's Poetry for the People, I began to explore and learn about the writing that is kept out of the canon, often the most truth-telling, risky and fundamentally urgent. Out of this tradition, I became a WritersCorps teacher and worked with youth of all ages, from twelve-year-olds running around the recreation room in Mercy Housing to continuation school students in their late teens. I experienced firsthand the crucial importance of arts education to offer youth the tools with which to critically engage the landscape of their minds and communities.

Teaching with WritersCorps made me more fully invested in working towards a more just and empowering education system and society, as only listening to the stories of these students could. I do not think it will ever be possible to write without considering my former students as the potential readers and critics. Being a teaching artist galvanized my belief that writing can be a powerful force for change in ourselves and our communities.

Strawberries

> Abuelito, you once told me the plastic sheets
> used to seal in pesticides, stretching across acres
> were actually ocean waves touching down on our valley.
> I'd dream the bright reflecting cover
> was an outlawed slip and slide
> you laughing at the bottom with arms outstretched—
> but as you grew thin and mom repeats
> *memorize his face*

listen when he takes you to the fields
tattoo his voice on your ear drums
my dreams shift to dark scenes of agua de fresa
rotting upon contact with my tongue.
You, Abuelito, shake off white particles
    methyl bromide
    methyl bromide
burns through your skin
reveals your future dia de los muertos skeleton
your boney fingers snatch a strawberry from my mouth
disintegrating instantly with your bones
as I scoop heaps of ashes   looking for you in them.

Perhaps I am too old now to trace
Salinas strawberry roads in search of you
know I cannot kiss your deep tanned cheek
cannot ask what dawn looks like as it breaks
and brightens the rows upon rows you combed
in search of just-ripe berries
but I still search the tight bends and dust
still seek your leather palms
raising earth to my small fingertips.
I can still hear you explain
if it is dark   it is rich
if it crumbles   the roots can take.

I still see you pull down the sky
to show me thick clouds
so I can remember
when early rain comes
strawberries carry
brown spots on their backs
get tilled under
and their soil-like hands
push up against
plastic
and wait.

Prunedale, CA

We former Steinbeck Okies
former plum farmers
former trailers an' white trash
We headlights leading the way like
lighthouses an' hand-drawn maps
We set up camp in Hoovervilles
an' sing sizzlin' union hymns round the fire

We busted up trucks rust
where all the spiders nod off to sleep
poverty lawn furniture with daddy sayin'
>   *soon as I get some extra money*
>   *I'll fix 'er up an' sell 'er off*
an' kids who don't know better   yet
an' sweep away the cobwebs
with the candy red paint of their minds

Now property prices on the rise
Mama sayin' things like
>   *land rich an' dirt poor*
an' three generations later
we see dirt bloom money
the ghosts of orange and lettuce crate labels
with *work as far as the eye can see*
get us ready to cross the stateline
as headlights hang from real estate signs
leadin' us back to Oklahoma, Arkansas
an' Nebraska
Cuz when rich folks want our homes
the family pets buried under the oak tree
an' our lil' handprints in the driveway's concrete
>   don't mean much
to the pitch of an empty stomach

We apron strings tied tight/rough hands
massagin' coarse dough/none of us really want
to ask why money keeps comin' up short an' none of us
have the heart to tell mama

snicker doodles out our old porcelain stove
taste better at Christmas
than a store bought present
with the brightest bow

Chrissy Anderson-Zavala studied and taught poetry in June Jordan's Poetry for the People at U.C. Berkeley. She is a Xicana writer from Salinas, California, and holds a B.A. from U.C. Berkeley and an M.A. in education from Stanford. She is one of the co-founders of *Common Language*, a multicultural feminist literary journal in partnership with Aunt Lute Books.

Cathy Arellano

My first memory of writing—because I wanted to, because I thought I had a story to tell—is when I was around ten years old. I was sitting in one of our two bedrooms on Guerrero Street. Nana, Grandpa, and Uncles Bobby and Tommy lived next door— next door behind-the-wall, not next door as in the next building. Auntie Rita lived on top of our ceiling in the flat that she took over from Uncle Joe. I sat listening to four lanes of cars speeding by and started writing excitedly, happily. After a while, I stopped myself when I realized—or remembered—that there were no books about girls, brown girls, brown girls who lived with extended family, without two parents in the same house, on a busy street, girls who liked other girls. Mission High's Mr. Ruffner and his daily journal entries, as well as bringing in Barrett Watten from California Poets in the Schools, brought me back to writing just in time: I had fallen in love with one of my best friends. I ended up putting away those journals until my mother passed away during my first year of college. I started writing again and haven't stopped.

When I joined WritersCorps, I knew I wanted to work in the Mission District of San Francisco. I wanted to provide young people from my neighborhood a form and a place to express what needed to get out. This resulted in readings, slams, publications, a play and, hopefully, more than I can imagine. Much thanks to the youth of Everett Middle School, Mission High, Mission Girls, Loco Bloco, Mission Cultural Center's Summer MAS Program, and the Girls After School Academy for taking a chance on themselves and me. And thanks to everyone who works with youth and works creating progress in this world.

Out With the Family

Circa 1991

Nana and I have been watching TV all night. First, the local news on channel 7, then Peter Jennings delivers the World News before Nana switches to *Wheel of Fortune*. She likes figuring out the puzzles before the contestants. Nana became a fan of Merv Griffin, the creator of the game, when he kept her company with his daily talk show while she cooked dinner for the army of her family. Later when Merv visited Grandpa and the other patients at Laguna Honda Hospital, Nana fell in love forever. At least, that's how she looks in that photo. Merv's pale hand is around her shoulder and Nana's brown-as-her-beans skin glows against his rosy cheek. They're leaning into each other like a happy couple. When friends see that photo, I tell them, "Look, it's Nana and Grandpa Merv." There's a photo of her and my real Grandpa on Market Street in the late 1930s, in black and white, framed with a thick white border. They are side-by-side but not touching. It looks as if they have been caught mid-stride. Grandpa's eyes look straight at the camera as if saying to the photographer, "Take the picture, asshole, then get out of my way." Nana's eyes are looking straight down.

Nana pushes 4-8 and we watch part of an old Mexican movie on Telemundo. Tonight, it's just Nana and me and it feels better than it ever did during childhood. Back then, more than half of her nine children and bunches of grandchildren constantly needed her attention, wanted some of her beans, or deserved her reprimand. I'm glad to have Nana all to myself, but I still feel a little shy at times. She comes across *Jim Thorpe, All American* and sets down the remote on the table by her side.

Tonight, there's no staring at beautiful strangers at Club Q, G-Spot, or The Box for me. It's San Francisco's gay pride weekend, and I'm home with my grandmother. I didn't plan it, but Auntie Diz called and asked me if I'd stay home with Nana so she could have some time off. Of course, I said yes. It's been harder than usual lately because Nana isn't talking to her again. Uncle Tony lives with his mother and sister, but Auntie doesn't ask him. She knows that Uncle's evenings off are sacred for him. I know that they'll probably meet up at Bal's or The Double Play near his job at Hostess or The Five or Dovre Club near the house. They're grown adults, but they don't drink in their home with Nana. No one does unless it's New Year's or a family party. Nana has disapproved of drinking, especially at home, since Grandpa used to beat her during his many rampages.

Auntie told me that Nana probably wouldn't eat much for dinner, but I brought her two enchiladas from Taquería El Toro on 17th Street and she ate both of them. Nana even asked me to make her a Pepsi float for dessert. Told me to help myself and I did. Everything—beans, Oreos, chorizo, pan dulce—tastes better at Nana's house. It's been that way since I was a kid and we'd come next door to her flat for a midnight snack at 8.

We finish our floats and the front door opens and closes. I'm surprised that Auntie Diz has come home so early, then I hear Uncle Tony's heavy footsteps come up the stairs and down the hall. He stops outside the living room door. Nana and I look away from Jim to say hi to Uncle but he's not there. We look back at Jim.

"BOO!" Uncle yells.

Nana and I jump even though we know he's been standing there.

"Want some chow mein?" He asks with an easy smile holding up a clear, plastic bag with white, Styrofoam to-go boxes inside. His eyes are so bloodshot that I half expect his optic nerves to shoot red lightning bolts like a crazed toy. He must have come from Kenny's, his current favorite hangout on South Van Ness near 16th, a Chinese restaurant connected to a bar that caters to prostitutes, their dates, drug dealers and other neighborhood folks.

"Hi, Ma. How's it goin', ol' grey mare?" Uncle says as he crosses in front of Nana in her chair. "How's it goin' Cath?"

"We're fine, Tony. Sit down and watch the movie," Nana tells him even though he is already on his way to sitting next to me on the couch.

"Hi, Uncle."

He sees Burt Lancaster.

"What's Moses doing?" he asks me with a thumb curved at the screen.

"It's Burt Lancaster. He's Jim Thorpe," I tell him.

"Who?"

"Lancaster, from *Eternity*," Nana clarifies.

"*Eternity*? What the hell?"

"*From Here to Eternity*, Uncle," I clarify.

"Who's he supposed to be if he's not Moses?"

"Jim Thorpe, the Native American athlete," I tell him.

"Oh! Those crackers fucked that Indian over!" he says wickedly while nodding his head with closed eyes and pointing at the screen.

"Tony, don't tell us what happens."

"What do you mean don't tell you? Everybody knows those assholes fucked him over and took his medals," he says indignantly looking at me. "You went to college. You know that, right Professor?"

"Yeah, well, I never took a Native American Studies class, but—"

"So, how ya been? How's school?" He asks loudly over the movie, as if it weren't even on and we weren't even watching it.

"I graduated."

"She graduated, Tony."

"I know. I was there. I just thought The Professor might have gone back to brush up on her shit. What'd you study? Or, uh, what was your major?" he asks with a fake serious look.

"English and History."

"History? And you don't know about Jim Thorpe? Are you telling me that I know more than The Professor?"

Usually, when I visit and he's sober, he ignores me. I don't hear him talk much to anyone. When we arrive, he nods hello or holds his hand up to say hi. If he's eating something and wants to share, he'll look at us and point at the food. When we get ready to go, he nods or holds up his hand again. When he's been drinking though it's hard to keep him quiet. I feel myself getting warm. When I look at him, he's sitting up and looking directly at me with the widest grin.

"Yeah, you know more than I do, Uncle."

"Aw, go to hell!" He waves for me to turn back to the TV and I do. Uncle looks back at the screen too.

Even with Burt Lancaster playing the lead role, Jim Thorpe's story is more interesting than I expected. Jim didn't want to go to the Carlisle Indian School. He went and wasn't happy until he became involved with sports. He won gold medals at the 1912 Olympics but after they're taken away he plays pro baseball, then football. I try to remember that it's just a Hollywood movie. A commercial for musical hits from the 1950s comes on.

"Someone to watch over me . . . " the TV croons.

I feel Uncle looking at me.

"Your mother loved that song," he tells me. He scoots up and stares at the TV before turning to Nana, "Didn't she, Ma?"

"I don't know Tony. Mono liked a lot of music," Nana responds. "Frank Sinatra, mariachis, those colored singers."

"Yeah, she liked a lot of different music, but I know she liked him. John-neee . . . Mathis. That's who sings that song." He remembers something and chuckles to himself.

"Remember the Fickle Fox?" he asks me.

"Fickle Fox? What's that?"

"You know, uh, Mission Playground?"

"Where Nickel Pool is?" I ask him.

"Yeah, Nickel Pool, Mission Playground, same thing. You remember Jets that used to be there on Valencia?"

I can see the large 1 and 9 lit up by dozens of clear light bulbs. Jets advertised their 19 cent fries with those blinking lights.

"Yeah."

"Remember across the little street from Jets there was a bar? The little street not Valencia."

I see the bar with a smiling red or dark orange fox face on a white background.

"Yeah, yeah, I remember." I can see Jets and Fickle Fox. I'm happy to share this memory with Uncle. Jets was torn down for the park's expansion and Fickle Fox has turned into a trendy tapas bar.

"Well, I was walking to Mama's, I mean Nana's, one day after work and I passed by that damn place."

I picture Uncle in his tan Derby jacket, white T-shirt, and Levi's casual slacks.

"I look and who do I see?"

He looks at me to guess. I have no idea and don't guess.

"Fucken Johnny Mathis!"

"Cool! Did you tell my mom?"

"Yeah, I told her that he was in there. She was surprised, 'Aw, Tony!' It was a bar for, uhm, gays."

Oh no. Gay is one word that does not get mentioned in Nana's or any family member's house. Growing up surrounded by 49ers Faithful and Raiders Haters, the only time I heard anything remotely "gay" was when my uncles watched their cross-bay rivals demolish the homeboys in red and gold on the football field. "Faggot Plunkett!" "Throw an interception, faggot!" "Sack his faggoty ass!" When I was a kid and still figuring out my gayness, I wondered how they knew Jim Plunkett was gay. Without attracting their attention, I studied him in his silver and black. Was it the way he ran? The way he threw?

Nana looks at Uncle then back to Jim. I look back at Jim.

"Did you know it was a gay bar?" he asks me.

"Nah, I had no idea. We used to just go to the playground to get our free lunches and swim."

"Tony, we're trying to watch the movie," Nana scolds him.

"I'm just trying to talk to my niece, Ma."

We're all quiet for a while.

"Hey, I ran into Auntie Dizzy earlier tonight at the Dovre Club."

I came out to Auntie last year. She held me as I told her that I wanted to be with Carla, one of my best friends. I told her that Carla used to tell me her fantasy about us living together and me cutting my hair and renaming myself Carlos. That she was going to become a lawyer and support me while I wrote poems all day. Then she got pregnant in our senior year and married the baby's father. She loved her daughter but complained about her husband and married life whenever we talked. And when I slept over, she put him on the couch and asked me to sleep with her. I told Auntie that I had been in love with Carla for years. That in eleventh grade, Mom had even asked me, "Are you in love with that girl?" I told Auntie that I had finally told Carla that I was in love with her and wanted to take care of her and her daughter. That Carla had said yes to being with me then backed out when I wanted to celebrate and take her out to a club, a dyke club. After hearing me talk through tears and cry through talking, Auntie shhh-shhhd me into falling asleep on the couch. Auntie had been very supportive of my queerness since that day, but I asked her not to tell anyone in the family.

"Yeah, she told me you're going to be selling sodas tomorrow."

"Mm-hm," I pretend to focus on the movie.

"What's the group raising the money for?" he asks.

"A retreat," I answer truthfully but not completely.

"You all go off in the woods or some shit like that?"

I've never been on a retreat—let alone a lesbian retreat—and am kind of unsure myself.

"I guess whatever everybody decides they want to do."

Please, God, make him pass out.

"Just women in the woods?" he asks.

"Tony, you have to go to work in a few hours. Why don't you go to bed so we can watch this movie in peace?"

"Aw, fuck work. Cath'll call me in. Won't you, Cath?"

I've heard him ask Nana, Auntie Rita, Auntie Diz, and some of my cousins to call in for him. I don't feel like doing him any favors, but no one has ever said no.

Jim catches the ball and runs past defender after defender. I wish I were Jim, running and running. I'd run past the goalpost and just keep going. I sneak a look at Nana. She's watching Jim.

"It's a lesbian group, Ma. They're gonna sell sodas at the gay parade for their lesbian retreat," he says casually as if he were announcing last week's football score.

I stop breathing. My eyes widen. I try to blink them back to normal size. My eyelashes are the only things moving. Nana sits frozen for a full minute. The announcer announces that we will take a break for their sponsors before returning with the final scenes. Finally, Nana scoots up in her seat and very carefully removes her glasses. She folds them and puts them in her cushioned pouch. She picks up each puzzle book and folds each cover back to the front. She picks up her pill containers from the side table. She puts the objects in her bag that hangs across her walker.

"She's a lesbian, Ma," Uncle chuckles.

Nana continues with putting her things away.

He tilts his head back against the couch and exhales as if he is exhausted.

"Ah, what the fuck. It's your own damn business, your own damn business," he mumbles more to himself than to me.

Jim returns. Nana and I watch him throw a football to a group of young boys. "THE END" covers Jim before the screen fades. A cubic zirconium commercial comes on then one for a little machine that dices, slices, and chops carrots. Nana turns to me.

"Are you staying the night, Cath?"

"Uh, no. No, Nan, I'm gonna go home when Auntie gets back."

"He's here," she points at Uncle with her long, brown finger. "You don't have to wait for her. She comes in late."

"That's okay, Nan. I'll wait."

"Do you have your car?"

"Mm-hm."

"Well, you know where the blankets are if you decide to stay or wanna lay down, right?"

"Ah-huh, yeah."

"Okay. Good night and be careful if you go home tonight."

"Okay, Nana, good night," I say a little too fast. I don't look at her, but I start breathing again.

"Tony, get some sleep before you have to get up for work in a few hours."

Nana waits but Uncle appears to have finally passed out.

She dismisses him with a wave of her hand. Then she pushes herself along with her walker and out the door. He opens one eye.

"Did the ol' grey mare leave?"

"Yeah." I have no idea what he's going to say next if anything.

"Whatever the hell you do, don't ever act like your shit don't stink."

My shit don't stink? This is what he usually accuses his recent ex-wife of: "She acts like her shit don't stink!"

"Okay, Uncle, I won't." I answer quickly to end the conversation.

"There's this asshole who comes to the bar and he always acts like his damn shit don't stink. I hate that asshole and it don't got nothin' to do with him being . . . that way."

Uncle knows a gay man. He knows about me. He knows—drinks with?—a gay man. This is my chance to ask him about Jim Plunkett.

"Okay, I'll try not to . . . uh, Uncle?"

"Hunh?"

"Uh, how did you know that Jim Plunkett is gay?"

"What? What the hell are you talking about?"

"Well, I remember hearing you and Uncle Tommy and Uncle Bobby talking about him whenever he was on TV. You guys were always saying, 'Fucken Plunkett, fag—"

He cuts me off.

"I gotta go to bed. Call my job. The number's on that paper near the phone. Tell them I might be 15 minutes late, but I'm coming in."

"Okay, Uncle." I guess open discussion time is over.

"Get $20 outta my wallet for a cab for you to go home," he says as he takes his wallet from his right back pocket and sets it on the couch's armrest.

"Thanks, Uncle, but I have my car."

"What'd I tell ya? Don't act like your shit don't stink. Take the damn twenty," he points at his wallet.

"But I have—"

"Take it for gas money then, goddammit."

"Okay, thanks."

"Damn kids think they know everything. Didn't even know who the fuck Jim Thorpe was. Brings up that asshole Plunkett. Lemme go to sleep."

He busts me out to Nana and now *he's* mad at *me*. I don't say anything else.

He gets up and walks to his bedroom. I call the Hostess office and pass on his message. I watch TV with the sound very low. I flip channels for a couple hours. I try to imagine how it will be the next time I see Nana. Finally, I reach for his wallet. As I do, I look down the hall to try to prepare myself in case of another "Boo!" I take out a twenty and put it in my own wallet.

Soon after, he opens his bedroom door and walks down the hallway to the kitchen. He calls Yellow Cab and orders a ride. He goes into the bathroom. I hear him wash up and brush his teeth. Then he walks into the living room and stands in the doorway.

"Did you get the twenty?"

"A-huh."

He crosses to the couch, picks up his wallet, and returns it to his back right pocket. He nods good-bye and walks down the hall without saying anything else. He returns to the doorway. I'm surprised that he's back and look up.

"Plunkett isn't gay. He's a fucken traitor. I don't like him cuz he played like shit for the Niners for two years then he signed with the Raiders and won two them fucken Super Bowls."

He turns around and walks back down the hallway. His footsteps are much lighter on the stairs than when he entered a few hours earlier. I feel the cold wind as I hear the door close. I swim through channels until I find *Saturday Night Live* perform a *Family Feud* skit.

Cathy Arellano is the author of the chapbook *I Love My Women Sometimes They Love Me*. A San Francisco Mission District native, she is on extended leave in Burque's South Valley and teaches at the University of New Mexico and Central New Mexico Community College. She writes about "growing up brown, coming out queer, and living as true as I can which is kinda crooked."

Paola Corso

© Michael Winks

My writing is set in the Pittsburgh river town where my Italian immigrant family found blue-collar work. The poetics of witness is a phrase that has been used to describe my writing, and so I have begun to see myself as a witness to my family's working lives and struggles in a city yet to fully rebound from industrial decline. But Pittsburgh is a city of rivers and bridges. I think of its golden spans and flow of the river. I draw from oral histories and folklore to create magical leaps, a bend in the story open to possibility.

I led creative writing workshops at Bronx-Lebanon Hospital and a senior center in the Belmont neighborhood with WritersCorps. I'll never forget one woman who came every week but chose not to share her writing with the group. Willie Lou had never graduated from high school and worried about her spelling and grammar. I saw how she clutched her notebook close to her bosom and knew that some of us would be self-conscious or be writing close to the bone. I worked to create a safe house for our stories.

Then, one day, another participant read a poem about being molested by a family member. That was the day Willie Lou lowered her notebook on the table and read from it. She blossomed after that. When participants gave a reading to celebrate the literary journal we published, her daughter took off work to hear her mother so poised and confident as she recited her poems into the microphone. It was the graduation party Willie Lou never had. She set an example for us all to believe in ourselves and our stories.

Step By Step With The Laundress

1. It's easier to wash clean clothes if wearing clean clothes,
a saying adapted from your college-educated uncle who says it's
easier to find a job if you have a job when he hears you chewed
out Stubby for cutting back your hours at Eat'n Park.

2. Sort clothes in neat piles on the basement floor beside the safe
where your loud father Mister Twenty Horns stashes company photos
from mill picnics and prayer cards for every deceased member
of the goddamned family, alphabetized by saint.

3. Check pockets for matches, lighters, cigarettes left from break, a string of beads Unc bought for job interviews but you wore to bar bingo and stuffed in a pocket because it felt like bugs around your neck.

4. Load the washer, set the dial, and pour in double the detergent, knowing Mister Twenty Horns waters it down since you told him to either stop buying the cheap-ass Giant Eagle brand or you'd quit doing his laundry.

5. As soon as the clothes are submerged in soapy water, have a cigarette and listen to Tom Jones until he skips on the line "Whoa, whoa, whoa, she's a lady" or your butt burns out. Whichever comes first.

6. When the load begins to agitate, drink your coffee on the porch beside your grandmother's scrub board and hand wringer that Mister Twenty Horns will make you use if his water bill gets any higher from trying to get mill soot out of his work clothes and the soup of the day off yours.

7. Hang a taut line. Keep a clothespin in your mouth as if smoking a cigarette while your work friend Donna finishes your hoagie because her daughter ate hers and you gave yours up for adoption.

8. Group clothes and hang together with one exception. Don't put your 36 D hooter holders next to Donna's 32 AAA because Mister Twenty Horns will figure out you've been washing her clothes since she got fired and kick your ass all the way to a laundromat.

9. Have a cigarette on the porch while the clothes dry. Then check on your dying uncle next door as soon as your father stops yelling about you getting another pay cut at Eat'n Park so you'll never get the hell out of his house.

10. Get rid of the wasp nest near the line because Twenty Horns is too cheap to hire an exterminator and says you'll blow them away with your smoker's cough. You tell him you smoke like a chimney but he breathes in what the stacks at the mill belch out so he'd get lung cancer first anyway.

11. Take clothes down from the line then see if you can go offer to change your uncle's pillowcase next door because it's moist from his shallow breath and you suddenly need him to see you wearing the beads he gave you, if he remembers why.

12. Fold the clothes. Out of respect for your uncle, plan to wear a clean uniform from the basket if you need to visit the funeral home then go straight to work at Eat'n Park rather than call in sick. You want to believe what he told you.

Hole

The laundress picks up a shovel and starts digging. She tries
not to think about missing her uncle's funeral 'cause Stubby

changed her work schedule at the last minute and told her
to come in early to fill in for Marla May who called in sick

at the last minute when she woke up in bed with a tickle
in her throat and Stubby woke up with a tickle in his cock

beside her. She digs a hole one foot deep, wants to forget how
she smoked two packs yesterday and burnt the chicken nuggets.

She kept them in oil so she could picture Stubby's balls breaded
and browned to a crisp, knowing some old lady with no teeth

was gonna complain. She digs a hole two feet deep and hopes
her father doesn't come home early and find out what she's

about to bury in his yard. She digs a hole three feet deep
and knows what he'd say if he noticed a fresh mound of dirt

and she'd say she weeded to plant flowers. She digs a hole four
feet deep and since when did she give a damn about flowers

when she yanked every blooming thing in sight so she wouldn't
have to smell something sweet instead of her cigarette smoke.

She digs a hole five feet deep and remembers when she bought
her mother a corsage for her silver wedding anniversary party

because she deserved to smell something besides all his shit
for 25 years. She digs a hole six feet deep, puts down her shovel,

wraps a blanket around Donna's puppy, puts a garbage bag over it,
sets it in the grave. Donna lives in an apartment and didn't know

what to do with it like the laundress doesn't know what she's going
to do with the white carnation she bought to lay on her uncle's coffin.

She smells the flower then tosses it down the hole. She buries
the blackness with her last shovel of dirt and still sees white.

Paola Corso is a New York Foundation for the Arts poetry fellow and Sherwood Anderson Fiction Award winner. She is the author of *Giovanna's 86 Circles*, a John Gardner Fiction Book Award finalist, and a book of poems, *Death by Renaissance*, both set in her native Pittsburgh. Most recently, she and Nandita Ghosh co-edited *Politics of Water: A Confluence of Women's Voices*, a special journal issue published by Routledge Press.

© Bayete Ross Smith

Myron Michael Hardy

I'm a poet who sings songs that are some-
times rap, sometimes spoken word, and other
times traditional verse. To me the process of
writing is as important as the product of writ-
ing. As a poet and teacher of poetry, I believe
it's necessary for a poet to be aware of as many processes and kinds of
poetry as possible; this increases a teacher's ability to reach students
where they are, in terms of their understanding and practice of poetry.
Some students like structure; if given a traditional form—such as a
ghazal, sonnet or pantoum—they find greater expression within the
structure of the form. Other students like free verse and when given
a traditional form they wall themselves out of an open space. They'd
much rather have the entire page as their canvas. And then there are
students with a knack for storytelling, and it is no surprise that they
find their voices in the prose poem. When I teach a student how to
understand and write poetry at a deeper level, how to implement a
process to document that understanding and practice, I believe I'm
relearning my own understanding and practice of writing, and for this
we are all better poets.

In 2007, during my first year as a WritersCorps teaching artist at
Log Cabin Ranch, a high school for incarcerated young men, a student
of mine had a hard time writing a poem. He said it was because he
couldn't write as fast as he thought and therefore couldn't capture the
best poetry he was capable of writing. He was an emcee, and emcees
are the poets of hip-hop and "freestyle," which is another word for
what André Breton and his cadre of surrealist homies called the trance-
like practice of "automatic writing." So I bought a mini tape recorder,
turned it on, and told my student to throw his fear into the pond be-
hind the library. After each session, we listened to his freestyle, then he
transcribed it into compelling written poetry, a flow caught on paper.

Vanity Fair

driving towards nothing natural, an heirloom
of disastrous hand-me-downs from grandfather to father's
cousin to kin, skin deep in rim-washed white walls spinning
going where a question mark shapes place demarcated
on a grid with a slump   period   the things we shelve higher

than self in our taking to safe keep a poof of air, ash and rust
a gust of wind and it's all gone, overtime water transforms
if wheels meet the lake, stop spinning and wait to be craned out
if wheels meet the road, pothole a weak axel, a problem
the engine and transmission stall, the nails and bolts of wind
in a bottle, the sail of a boat floating in the middle of nowhere
else cares the kid with a slinky, a fist is made it doesn't
climb a ladder of wooden stairs, stubborn things like human
    beings
stuck in the crook of a cul-de-sac, minds bent on a point, vanity
fairs where hats come off, off they go
platinum smiles then piles of bones, hats blowing in the wind
strangers and lovers scrambling to catch them, arms akimbo
growing like trees in a wasteland, shelves for things that cost life,
death and taxes, a man working a pipeline spits

The Untree

There is a song in my head I can't stop singing
where *the sky is falling in*, it wrings water
from a towel. I'm soaked
from having walked six miles in the rain. Nowhere
easier than going downhill, this place, the Untree.
The inhabited, *X marks the* grave, marks the first
and last of our crossing, our passing
books on shelves, artists carrying a canvas
browned with iodine. *I'm up in the clouds,*
I'm downtown where loud speakers thump
and dinosaurs slump in garbage bins, I'm spinning
everything I've owned in an ethereal loom
to avoid evanescence; the gap widening
the space between us. You're off and involved
in the business of becoming; *I'm up in the clouds,*
staring, wearing quasi-wet clothes, *parting*
the waves of people throwing themselves
hand and foot at life. *Where I end you begin*
to make our first crossing the last offering
my name in your mouth. *I'm up in the clouds,*
you've forgotten my name. I can't stop singing,

can't leave you alone. How *you left me*
hungry for your laughter, hungry for limelight.

Hail to the thief, I will eat you alive.

But *I can't come down*, I can't round a corner
and find shelter at home. I gather poems
like lyrics don't matter if names like notes
aren't soaked in rain. *You left me alone*, dressed
in the dark, I molded sheets into your shape
to feel the space you left warm. *I'm up in the clouds*,
I'm down in the dark, looking for sparks
where I end and you start. No more lies,
no more lipstick. *X marks the place*, the Untree,
our first and last crossing. *I'm up in the clouds*,
where *the sky turns green*, and he is moving
his things into your car. And there's a song
in my head I can't stop singing, *Hail to the thief*.
In time, providence gives one peace, *I will eat
you alive.* But *I'm up in the clouds
and I can't come down*, and the rain won't let up,
and his clothes are in your car. *And I'm sorry
I'm sorry* for going where she went
and laughing at her jokes and roping off her life
with all my energy. *I'm sorry for us*, the Untree.
The X that marks the grave, the books
on shelves, the artists carrying a canvas
dodging curbs and cars, *where I end and you start*.

Myron Michael Hardy is a poet and recording artist. He curates and hosts Heliotrope, a monthly reading series in San Francisco and is the sole proprietor of Rondeau Records. His songs are featured on *Songs of Experience*, *Masters Thesis* and *Transit Belongings*, and his poems have appeared in several literary journals. He earned an M.F.A. in writing from California College of the Arts and lives in Oakland, California.

Kim Nelson

© Amy Nelson

I am moved and marked by teaching incarcerated youth. I believe in the power of writing to reveal the meaning of our lives. I was deeply inspired working with young men who had "fallen" and had the courage to look at themselves through their writing. The process by which creativity transforms pain compels me, and I witnessed many occasions of students gaining understanding about what they'd been through, and finding more potential for their future. Their stories were the currency of our relationship, and we exchanged and listened more closely to each other than is usually undertaken in everyday life.

Because their lives were extraordinary, so were these exchanges. They were greatly relieved to learn how to write and to say what they really wanted to say. This exchange process forged strong connections, and I made good friends whom I value and miss. I chose to be non-judgmental, very present and grounded in the process of creativity with language as my medium. I was excited by the respect for oral traditions evident in their language as well as by the disrespect for intellectual distance. I remain dedicated to incarcerated youth—their education, artistic opportunity, equity and freedom.

Time Like This

As we round a long curve
on Highway 17
my tall two and a half year old
questions me
from the dark back seat.

Have you ever killed someone?

I realize in the end it is good he asks
for this war is all around,
it is good he is not sure
I am part of it.

I know I am every mother as I watch him sleep.
I feel their ghosts
and the hungry shadows of children

not safe cast about
our daily lives.
Here—hands finger his books in the basket.
There—in the steamy mirror as I dry his fresh skin,
tugging—at the corners of the blanket in the dim night-light.
Mommy, what if you bleed all the way out?

Many women lie awake
ache with news
closing in.
Many roll to sleep
helpless
in this darkness
and still dream.

Another day.

This is my sad earth.
This is our old sky.

The Gambler's Granddaughter

There is a moment in the song
words in my forehead
melody lilting over my breastbone
where my pulse rests with its rhythm
and I fall inside, major to minor chord
through the open window, into those righteous 7 semi-tones.

Rocking, rocking, chair, now still—
listening like an old telephone operator
to the searching crackle before the connection's made—
I hear my grandmother work
after grandfather'd lost in a poker game.
How my father learned his mother, at the piano
then his daughter, like a new musical pattern—the perfect fifth—
when she went to work.

I know the noisiness of women.
Their love thick as dahl soup
sustaining—a balm of lifetimes—

said to be invisible
as wrinkles ironed flat
seduced into the heat and steam.

I know the silence too, the slow demand
the secret, the diet, the headache and make-up
the dance the drink the smoke
the blood of the watercolor
the sealing kiss, and the veil

thrown off and most free
in that wave of wrist to God
that stellar intent to reveal
an open face to love with
or shirk of tradition
a pulling back of hair to tend a child.

This love has never been quiet,
the shift to a minor key
with that bell intention,
from a necessary and lovely bower

from where the leaves fall
like butterflies
twisting in delicate surrender
to another's breath—
fall to the earth, a humble pile
gazing up at the expanse of
trunk and limb and fellow leaf
and toward each shining slice of sky
as it disassembles,
knowing this shifting dust.

I become, I become.

Kim Nelson taught WritersCorps workshops for nine years to young incarcerated men from San Francisco at Log Cabin Ranch. She co-hosted the *Poetry Show* on KUSP public radio in Santa Cruz and was the producer and co-writer of the short film *60 Seconds of Distance*, which cast former students from the Ranch. Kim is now working for The Beat Within, a weekly paper for incarcerated youth.

The Only War is the War Against the Imagination

© Joel Dias-Porter

Joel Dias-Porter (DJ Renegade)

I try to write poems that engage all the worlds I travel through. I love performing, so poetry slams were natural for me. I was living in the CCNV Homeless Shelter in downtown Washington D.C. in 1995, when I joined the newly created Writers-Corps. I had lived in the shelter for two years, which allowed me to spend my days in various libraries around town reading and studying poetry. I made most of my money doing small readings and poetry slams and selling handmade chapbooks. WritersCorps provided a way for me to make a slightly better living and still focus most of my time on studying, writing and performing.

I am proud of the fact that I was the very first writer/instructor ever hired into the program. I was already teaching my "From Rapping to Writing" workshop at Ballou High School, so it was a natural transition. Many of the workshops were gratifying on a personal level, such as the three years I taught at the medium-security facility at Lorton Reformatory. I have been many times to other prisons to visit my father, brothers and uncles, so I felt a kinship with my students there. The prisoners were always grateful for our presence, more so than at any other type of site where I taught.

Joining WritersCorps was important to me in terms of identifying myself as a writer and in being exposed to other writers. It also gave me a chance to give back to the inner-city neighborhoods which I came out of. One of my proudest moments was seeing one of our troubled former middle school students who had participated in WritersCorps activities all the way through high school get accepted into, and graduate from college.

Wednesday Poem

I pass through the metal detector inside
the front doors of Cardozo High,
with a folder of nature poems
and a lesson planned to introduce my students
to the pistil and stamen of the Wild Iris.
After signing my name in the visitor's log,
I bop down two flights of steps.

Outside the classroom things are too quiet
and Mr. Bruno (who's Puerto Rican and writes poetry)
takes ten minutes to answer the door.
There's a student snapshot in his hand.
One of our kids got shot last night,
Remember Maurice? Maurice Caldwell?
He didn't come to school much.
A Crisis Response Team has the kids in a circle,
and I've never seen them sit so quietly.
Every computer in the classroom is dead.
A drawing of Maurice is taped to the board,
a bouquet of cards pinned under it,
Keisha (who writes funny poems in class)
says Maurice would help her with Math,
she liked him but never told him.
The crisis lady says, *It's OK to cry.*
Keisha says she been ran out of tears.
Mr. Bruno tells me, *Somebody called him*
from a parked Buick on Thomas Place NW.
When he walked up, they fired three times.
I freeze. That's a half block from my house.
There are four crackhouses on that block
and I never walk down that street.
I wonder why he approached the car—
was he hustling crack or weed?
Or did he recognize the dude and smile
before surprise blossomed across his face,
and the truth rooted into his flesh?
His face flashes before my irises,
I see him horseplaying with Haneef,
his hair slicked back into a ponytail.
He wrote one poem this whole semester,
a battle rap between cartoon characters.
Mr. Bruno asks if I still want to teach.
I open my folder of xeroxed poems,
then close it, and slump in a chair.
What simile can seal a bulletwound?
Which student could these pistils protect,
here where it's natural for a boy
to never see seventeen?

Inaceo

I remember when men left Maio
to hunt whales,
to scoop oil from their heads for light.
I would sit in the harbor
and watch the ships drift out,
their sails swelling
like the shirts of hanged men.
The sea is the stingiest of lovers,
she has carried off my five sons
like driftwood.
I never learned to read Portuguese
but I can read the rocks in a field,
and tell you whether to plant corn or cane.
Sometimes we go years with no rain,
until the fields are covered
with as many bones as stones.
My bones know as much
about when the winds will change,
as the man in the radio.
I like the man in the radio,
he doesn't demand
that everything stop to look at him.
This afternoon we played *oril,*
Antonio joked that I can't drive a car,
but he can't drive a *burro.*
He says there are flowers beyond
these islands that I have never seen,
but there are things under these rocks
that he has never seen.
Here we have more rocks than flowers.
You don't water rocks
but neither do they die.
After carrying crops to market,
I still sit and watch the waves curl
until the sun dips into the sea.
My hat was worn by my father,
and shades my face as it shaded his,
but some things have changed.

Now light comes through wires.
On this island we have plenty light,
if you want to impress me, make it rain.

Mae Velha

for Cesaria Evora

Tonight, a barefoot woman
(who knows Melancholy's
middle name is Exile)
sings of ten brown crumbs
spotting the Atlantic's azure carpet.
Her voice, amber and aged
as a shot of fine scotch,
floats over our heads
like a *tchintchirote* over the waves.
With the ease of a girl
rinsing sea salt from her hair,
and the rhythm of a boy kicking
a ball of rolled up socks,
she sings of *Frutu Proibido*
known only to the night,
of *Destino Negro*
known only to the stars.
Sings of her sons in Holland working the docks
her daughters in America waiting tables.
Sings as if she too has tried
to fill an empty heart
with silver coins, or golden liquor,
has passed the hours
squinting at the horizon
for a familiar sail.
To the boy waiting for his father
she sings *Coragem Irmon*,
and to the girl waiting for her man
she offers *Consedjo*.
To a people whose only birthright
is a hot dusty wind
she is a black saint of both

morabeza and *despidida,*
blessing us
with a voice as moist
as sand after the sea's kiss.
And when there is no rain
the rhythm of her notes soak the soil,
when there is no grain
the syllables of her song fill our mouths.
And when we awake
in strange places
to find even the wind
whispering in a foreign tongue,
her voice is a vessel
returning us
to those ten rugged rocks
wrinkling the aqua silk of the sea.

Joel Dias-Porter (DJ Renegade)'s poems have been published widely, in places such as *Time* magazine and the *Washington Post*. He has performed on the *Today Show*, in the feature film *SLAM*, on BET's *Teen Summit* and in the documentaries *Voices Against Violence* and *SlamNation*. He competed several times in the National Poetry Slam, finishing as high as second place in the individual competition, and became the 1998 and 1999 Haiku Slam Champion.

© Larrie Lance

Mahru Elahi

My writing has its roots in the profound silences I experienced as a girl. Those silences burrowed deep into bone: divorce, the vilification of fellow Iranians, my freckled "passing" skin, rape. As a young person, putting pen to paper was one of the few acts where I felt any sense of control. With the encouragement of some dear teachers, I began to chisel away at the rock around my heart, to mold and shape my story into words that embraced others, that held mirrors up. Within two families and a larger culture that have few words for what I am, I now write myself into being. Words fill me, like the stuffing of a rag doll. Without them, I do not exist.

I began to think of myself as a writer during my junior year of high school. Most students didn't like our American literature teacher, Ms. Tiernan. They called her "Bulldog" because of the loose skin that cascaded down her cheeks. I would receive essays back from her dripping with red ink. Instead of being upset by all those crimson marks, I was energized. Here was someone who believed in me, who wanted to push my writing further. I tried to do the same for my students during the five years I was a classroom teacher in New York City public schools. I had entered the field of education because teachers like Ms. Tiernan had been so critical to my development.

WritersCorps was a natural step when I moved back to California in 2003. WritersCorps was a coming home, an affirmation of both my work as a writer and a mentor to youth. The program allowed my creative life to crackle and zip like grease in a frying pan. Doors opened onto a community of artists and writers whom I continue to work with, and learn from. Youth opened their lives to me: from Ida B. Wells High School to Sanchez Elementary School, from the Center for Young Women's Development to the city-wide WritersCorps youth intern program. I could hold hard truths, listen to stories that other adults might flinch at.

I wanted to capture some of the relationships I've developed over the years, in a medium that felt immediate and alive. The pages that follow began as an informal picture-journal.

THEA KEEPS A JOURNAL: "BLACK
INK IS NO SLAVE TO EMOTION/
BUT ONLY A HELPLESS SERVANT"
SHE WRITES LYRICS NOW, IN-
STEAD OF POEMS AND
WORKS AT GUITAR CENTER
THE FIRST TIME WE TALK-
ED WAS ON THE # 22.
I KNEW SHE WAS GLORIA'S
STUDENT, SAT ACROSS
FROM HER. SIX MONTHS
LATER, SHE WAS
TEACHING IN
MY CLASSES.
WHENEVER
SHE STOOD,
IT WAS
QUIET.

ME 2006

GIRL
THE DEAD MILKMEN

WHEN I SAW ROBERT SKANKING/
AT AN ALL-AGES SHOW/RICHOCHET-
ING OFF BODIES/GIRL BUDDY AT
HIS SIDE/MY MUSIC AND TEACH-
ING WORLDS HELD HANDS FOR
A FEW PRECI___OUS HOURS,
FINGERS INTER___LACED,
THEY POGO-ED/___FACE TO
FACE/FEET SMA___SHING
INTO THE FLOOR/___HEADS
SOARING SKYWARD/___ROBERT
WRITES/"... I HAVE N___O DREAM
HE MEANS/INJUSTICE
WHIPS TOWARD HIM
A SKATEBOARD
FOR PROTECTION
MAYBE A
PEN/SOME-
TIMES

ME
2006

UZI SUICIDE

ANNIE IS ONE OF THE BEST POETS
I KNOW. SHE WRITES A LOT ABOUT
RIDING THE BUS, "EXCUSE ME EX-
CUSE ME IS IN THE GESTURE OF MY
ARMS/SPACE IN BACK, NO ONE
MOVES" AND MAKES HER OWN ZINE
CALLED *nonsensical*.
ANNIE HELPED RE-KINDLE MY
INTEREST IN ZINE-MA
KING. I WAS CO-COOR
DINATOR OF THE INT
ERN PROGRAM THE
YEAR ANNIE PART
ICIPATED. IT
WAS A ROUGH
YEAR BUT WE
ALL GOT THR-
OUGH IT.

2001
ME

I FIRST MET ERIC FOSTER IN 2004.
HE WAS A TRANSFER FROM SOUTH SAN
FRANCISCO, A FOOTBALL PLAYER.
AT LUNCH HE WOULD SIT ALONE IN MS
LANGLOIS' ROOM, STARING OUT WIDE
WINDOWS TOWARDS GOLDEN GATE
PARK. HE SAYS THAT
HEARING ME READ
MY POEM 'OLOKUN'
MADE HIM WANT
TO WRITE HIS OWN.
HE HADN'T REAL-
IZED HOW POWERFUL
WORDS COULD BE. HE
STARTED CALLING HIM-
SELF A MESSENGER
AND PERFORMING ALL
OVER THE CITY. NOW
HE'S A NEWLYWED,
WRITING EPICS
WHEN HE CAN. — ME 2006

JESSICA IS BREAST FEEDING • I
NOTICED BABY-BANG FRINGE RING-
ING HER FOREHEAD, TOLD HER IT
LOOKED CUTE • SHE HADN'T PLANN-
ED IT THAT WAY • HAIR STARTED
FALLING OUT WHEN NYANNA WAS
BORN • IT'S GROWING BACK • LAST
YEAR SHE SAT WITH CRYSTAL
AND DI... N'T ALWAYS WANT
TO W... TE • NOW, EVEN
WHE... N SHE MISSES
CLA... SS, SHE MANAGES
TO FIND ME,
SAYS WHICH
TEACHER
SHE TALKED
BACK TO,
WHY SHE
FEELS BAD
ABOUT IT

ME
2006

Mahru Elahi is a writer and zine-maker. Her poetry was anthologized in *Let Me Tell You Where I've Been: New Writing by Women of the Iranian Diaspora* (University of Arkansas Press). She was awarded a Hedgebrook Residency, a B.A. in American studies from U.C. Santa Cruz and an M.S. in teaching from New School University. Her most recent work, *Blame It On Pluto*, is self-published online.

Thomas Centolella

Though I have taught at the college level for many years, much of my most satisfying teaching has occurred with young writers. While my writing has always had its rewards, my teaching has provided its own welcome complement. Fortunate teachers learn from their students (or at least are reminded, often in novel ways, of the fundamental veracities). My year in WritersCorps (1998-99) was spent with two very different populations under the roof of Newcomer High School in San Francisco. Newcomer serves as an opportunity for immigrant students to hone their English skills before joining mainstream schools. In 1998 Newcomer also provided classrooms for the debut of a new charter school, Gateway. My immigrant kids were Chinese, their English eccentric but workable.

One talented 16-year-old, an aspiring industrial designer, admired a piece of origami I'd improvised, a kind of tiny Mies van der Rohe chair. His comment: "Easy to do, hard to think"—a comment that could describe the nature of creativity. Accomplished art seems so self-evident, as if sprung whole out of thin air. But not everyone is privy to the vagaries of inspiration, and the problem-solving of the imagination. As for my Gateway freshmen, many were gifted but knew very little about poetry. By the end of the year, after turning in impressive poem after poem, they were clamoring to be included in the anthology I was assembling. Because no yearbook was planned, the kids used their anthology copies to commemorate their first year together—an appropriate enough gesture, since they had come to learn that the creative journey inward also led outward: into the community they themselves were making, and into the larger world they would never again apprehend in quite the same way.

Transparency

That year everything went transparent.
First the buildings. Their concrete and granite,
their monumental marble, all seemed like
cardboard facades one stiff wind would flatten.
Then faces. What they registered was never more fleeting,
and what astonishment lay hidden behind them—

space shuttle, sonata form, world series, mortal sin—
were, after all, only fabrications of flesh and blood:
perishable, pitiable, nothing more.
Worst of all was hope. Like wine
turned back to water, hope was weak
and easily seen through.

It was something of a miracle, then, that one day
when, dwarfed by the library's massive vault,
penned in by words intended for posterity,
I stared at the hand holding open my book
and saw it was only flesh and blood,
but perfect. The greenish veins, the knuckles
and grimy nails, the fine reddish blond hairs ablaze,
even the tiny white scar left by an army knife when I was
        seven—
my hand was nothing to be improved upon.

And I looked up from the book that had been failing miserably
to enlighten or uplift me, and among the dreary stacks
and institutional quiet, I was drawn
to human faces—each one holding the weight of a world
carefully chosen or acquired at random,
faces open to me now as any book—
and one by one, I began to read them.

Setsubun

The solar panels are up over the projects,
the edible dandelions sprouting yellow in the vacant lot,
clover coming up thick around the kitchen chair
where a two-story house once stood.

It's early February but the Japanese next door
say it's the end of the year. Spring, they say, has come
to rid the soul of last year's demons.
There's no Arctic blast to argue the point.

In my courtyard I smell lilacs
where there are no lilacs.

* * *

My demon called last week.
Just wanted to chat.
On a rainy night in late January
even demons get the blues.

Topic of discussion? Oh, this and that.
Couple of lame jokes, the usual news.
If you'd been there to eavesdrop, no doubt
you would have been bored.

With my demon, what goes unspoken
is what provokes.

* * *

Some days are like this: you can't move.
Can't be moved. As if you've put down roots.
What growth there is, is imperceptible.
A slow efflorescence.

Then the camellia, out of season,
blooms for you. The cherry trees bloom
like something you've been meaning
to remember. And the Japanese fern

which all winter was thought to be dying
shoots up a new green stem that spirals toward the light.

* * *

And other days: the window light woke me early
but I didn't mind. From the courtyard
I heard a trilling, intricate as my favorite jazz,
and half-dreamt that bird to be

the return of John Coltrane. A sweet
modulation, loopy, lively, it followed me out
the door, down the street, and around the corner:
like my mongrel, Errant, who would chase me to work,

then wander off for days—they seemed
a lifetime—but would always come back.

      * * *

The ingenious Japanese are making masks of terror
to mock the awful past, render it harmless.
I'll have to make do with my face
which is already a mask of intense equanimity.

Fumes of hot pitch in the air, and far off I can see
the construction cranes at Third and Mission.
They loom over the empty lot where Robért
lived rent-free for years, and well, in his condemned painter's
    loft.

You pulled a string in the mail slot; it connected
to a tin can at the top of the stairs: his doorbell.

      * * *

Next door at the end of the year: the heads
of sardines, hung from holly branches.
And parched beans, flung inside the house
and outside the house. "In with fortune, out with demons!"

Instead of fish and beans, I use disappointments
torn from an envelope, read quickly, discarded quickly.
I say it out loud—"It's all clear"—
like the reassuring signal after an enemy attack.

"Clear." As when the trauma surgeon with his electric paddles
jolts the cardiac victim back to life.

Thomas Centolella is the author of three books of poetry, all from Copper Canyon Press: *Terra Firma, Lights & Mysteries* and *Views From Along the Middle Way*. His awards include the National Poetry Series (selected by Denise Levertov), the American Book Award, the California Book Award in poetry and the Bay Area Book Reviewers Award.

Hoa Nguyen

Poetry is alive when it can exist in various contexts. It is a language of relating and a thing lived. During my two-year tenure with WritersCorps, I was paired with a ceramic muralist, and together we worked with first generation Southeast Asians in San Francisco's gritty Tenderloin District. Together we created tile murals while we investigated ghost tales, cultural and imagined blessing rituals and symbols, and created super hero figures. With a group of elders, we presented traditional Vietnamese folk-poems translated into English.

Our compositional methods could be improvisational, spontaneous, playful and "out there" (borrowing from the Surrealists and Oulipo); the results were often fantastic. The teens were sometimes delighted and often surprised by the works they created. Then later, a permanent mural would be installed in their neighborhood, in an alley next to the corner store. They could visit them any day. Words made real.

A youth anthology proposal was accepted that first year, and it was incredible to see how the young writers responded to their words in print: poem as object, another community expression. I continue to be engaged with bringing the poetry of others into print as a small press publisher; I also continue to teach writing workshops. There, each week, we spend an hour reading a source text aloud before writing for an hour in response to improvisational prompts. "Poetry is about continuing poetry," writes Joanne Kyger. I also believe that it can fight the war against the imagination, as Diane di Prima once said, "The only war is the war against the imagination."

Add Some Blue

1.

The mother says: ebola virus lives beneath fingernails
The mother waves yellow surveyor flags
The mother wears a gay shift   a shift of spirals

What to make of the century plant
    4 "babies" in a gravelly bed

You might naturally be a poet and feel a mosquito suck you
You might mix dried leaves and warm water for your hair

Dante rides his bicycle
        There's fire-wheel in the tall grass by the elm stump
                and a "Break the Bank" scratch off lottery ticket

Someone lost their maroon shorts   it's getting run over

2.

Thinking of Bernadette   trying to live without
money   having written three checks today
(food)   I'd rather trade but make no
"valuable" goods   there is no gold standard
as the value of money and Boggy Creek go
winding
        Regulation authorities come
into being   Laugh tracks behind
the simplest things like 2 men speaking
with boing-ing sound effects (radio)   Ate
ginger miso with buckwheat noodles bought
with inconvertible money   (where *are* my metals)
and backed by   as the French call it
"liberating power"

3.

They sell you what disappears   it's a vague "they"
maybe capital T   who are they and mostly
poorly paid in China

Why does this garlic come from China
It's vague to me   shipping bulbous netted white bulbs
Cargo doused with fungicide and growth inhibitor

What disappears is vague   I can't trade for much
I can cook   teach you cooking   ferment
bread or poetry   I can sell my plasma

They are paid poorly in Florida
picking tomatoes for tacos
Some CEO is surely a demon
in this poem

Need capital to buy   need to buy or else
you are always paying rent   one month away
from "the street"
3 neighbors asked for money this week
                We are guilty
bringing in sacks of food   bought on credit

Trademark this poem   mark this with a scan code
on the front and digitally store it somewhere
not to be memorized "by heart"

4.

Add some blue to it
                your eyes that can't see yet
add some blue there   Texas
a big car-fever as my blue
car fades   paint fades in the sun

Texas says "we're friendly"
It's midday and we hear cars
adding some blue
Make it a blue
highway to drive home
to the world's end

Blue can spell your name   I don't
know that yet either   wrapped up
in the snake's coil   and wipe my hands

You have all the blue a little bit of
blue   like a blue turtle
encased in red-blue   blue-red
the throbbing vein

Who will I be now
going through the blue door
    that is going through me

I need you descending
and giving breath
    I think I'm writing
    this blue to get to you

Hoa Nguyen was born in Saigon in the Year of the Fire Horse and raised in the Washington D.C. area. She is the author of several collections of poetry, including *Kiss a Bomb Tattoo* and *Red Juice*, both from Effing Press, and *Hecate Lochia* (Hot Whiskey Press). She co-edits *Skanky Possum*, a book imprint and poetry journal in Austin, Texas, and has been anthologized in *New American Poets* (Talisman), *Not for Mothers Only* (Fence Books) and *Black Dog, Black Night: Contemporary Vietnamese Poetry* (Milkweed).

Christopher Sindt

Poetry allows me to experience the world. It dismantles and revises the way things are known. My particular subjects seem to be the natural world and the human body, and I think I am drawn to them because, like most subjects, they are endangered and easily politicized.

Working with WritersCorps at Mission Annex taught me about language, translation, and the bridge between experience and the discovery of art and poetry. I worked with students from Chinatown and the Mission District, and the clash of cultures was tense, exhilarating, funny and powerful. The students were both naïve and wise in ways that shocked me at first; soon, I realized that great art comes from nurturing these extremes.

My time at WritersCorps was a turning point in my life: it turned my idea of teaching upside down (I learned so much more than my students did!), and it provided urgency and specificity to some vague notions I had about social engagement. In the dozen or so years since leaving WritersCorps, my interests in social and environmental justice have deepened. I teach at Saint Mary's College, which takes as part of its mission an awareness of the consequences of economic and social injustice and a commitment to the underprivileged. My poetry was also forever changed by the experience. In some ways, it has become smaller, more humble.

Beginning With a Line By Julia Kristeva

Add to these processes the relations
Of the fragmented body:
Add the relations and
fragment: the processes of
the field: poppies, delphinium, vetch:
they must be catching, little
mirrors: on Easter Sunday
in the fragmented

sun, it's time for
cool messages under blue oaks:
globe lilies stand around

with their burdens: irises reveal
their embarrassing frailty:
we must add to these processes
the relations between the partial
sight-lines forward and back:

flowers hate us but we can't stop
listening for their deaths
and resurrections: keep the fragments
when there is no listing, no lasting:
their bodies stand there looking
insolent and too busy: once,
there were no signs in the field:
now the field is ruptured.

Words for Moving Water

Bounded by willow, as is
the way in field guides: the river
channeling, ebbing, as a story

returns, roaring more, then
less, cascading and flattening: or,
between: the place

of a story: a man fishes, swims, falls
into, speaks from: or
a kind of mirror, found in pools

beside eddies, the other side of
the canyon rising, to view
the black phoebe as it skims

the surface, the hawk's distorted
arc: you are so clearly
in or out of the river, entirely

missing something that is
underneath, or even, in:
in other rivers, there might be

a god or headwater to speak
of, or a raft, or danger or
solitude: it may lead

somewhere: you may know it
in your words: *cataract, back-
flow, anabranch*; or float

through rapids or toward
a dam: the dusty smell of
blackberry, grey pines

softening the hillside, standing
beside for an instant, this one:
coming to an end, attainably:

my river doesn't roar,
it opens to its own
gravity, its exit, listens for
the slight gasp
in time, and fills—

Christopher Sindt holds a Ph.D. in English and a master's degree in creative writing from U.C. Davis. His poetry collection *The Land of Give and Take* was published in 2002, and his poetry has appeared recently in *nocturnes, Pool, Swerve* and *Xantippe*. He is an associate professor of English at Saint Mary's College, where he directed the M.F.A. program in creative writing from 2000 to 2007, and is currently associate dean of liberal arts.

Stephen Beachy

Recently I had lunch with a young man I worked with a dozen years ago, who told me that our writing and art programs saved his life. That's an easy answer to the question of how meaningful Writers-Corps was as work, and certainly more encouraging than the other kids I worked with, now adults, that I've seen wandering the streets homeless and mentally ill. There are so many paths that can lead us to a life on the streets and to lives that work for us or lives that don't. I'd had my own experiences of life off the grid, but it was illuminating to intersect so many alternative stories and visions. The homeless kids and runaways from Guerrero House, Hospitality House and Huckleberry House had learned so many ways that language could be a tool for survival. The truth might set us free, but an artful fiction might keep us out of jail. Paulo Freire wasn't kidding when he said that education was a two-way street. Never assume that what looks like suffering from the outside isn't a flight through the stratosphere, or that the choices that led to this place are occasions for regret. In my writing I try to capture the dizzying complexity of language and stories, and to dream up maps of outsider experience that couldn't really tell anyone how to get from point A to point B.

From the novella *No Time Flat*

Wade's father drove him to a different farm, to buy a bike. A uniform golden green covered the land there, like grass. This was a crop. They stood in the barn with the farmer and studied the bike in silence. The bike was simply green, yet they gazed and gazed upon the bike. There was some process of boredom and suffering in time required to facilitate the purchase of this bike. Finally, the farmer's twelve-year-old son came in. He was a teenager now, and too big. Wade's father and the farmer went outside to work out the details of the exchange. Wade blushed. He was terrified to be alone with a teenager, who had plucked a piece of straw from a dusty bale, and was chewing it. Wade did not believe that he would live to be so ancient and ferocious. The young man chewed thoughtfully and lost himself in the pleasure of chewing. Wade thought he was a delicious, impossible animal. He let Wade stare as if he was used to being adored. He patted the bike seat with affection and an obscene familiarity, and then sat on it to show Wade that it was just too small. Wade thought that the sparkling green banana seat was excited. The young man took the straw from his mouth and poked it into Wade's.

* * *

They came back a week later to complete the exchange. The son was nowhere in sight. Wade's father had to sit in the kitchen with the farmer; he hadn't yet endured enough lazy speech to justify the extravagance of the bike. The bike glittered, it was green. Wade walked out by the barn. The color of the crop was beautiful and intricate. He waded into it and it was higher than his knees. It was varied and shimmering, green, gold, green, gold. He chewed on straw and walked back into the trees, where a small stream flowed.

Out on the land, he saw someone walking, and he thought it must be the farmer's son. As the figure grew nearer, he realized the man was too tall. It was a stranger; he had been following Wade and decided to come get him perhaps. Wade stepped boldly into the light, lay down in the grassy plants, and closed his eyes. He thought the crop would be ruined, and this thrilled him. He thought the stranger would come and think that he was sleeping or dead, and touch him and wake him up. He thought that ants were going to bite him. It seemed he was waiting for years and years. He opened his eyes and sat up and peered through the trees, trying to locate the dark figure in the light.

* * *

Wade developed a fever and was kept home from school. It was on that day that a shooting occurred on the playground. A sixth-grade teacher and a girl were killed and two children were wounded. The man with the gun escaped, but was killed by the police later that evening outside of Mr. Tippy's Hamburger Restaurant.

The shooting had been on a Wednesday. School was cancelled for the rest of the week. The townspeople expressed their belief that broad daylight had become more terrifying than the middle of the night. The shooter was described on the news as a "frustrated loner" and psychologists explained that he must have been molested and humiliated in a school. They interviewed his elementary school mates to prove he hadn't been the most popular child. When he heard the term "frustrated loner," Wade felt that he would someday commit a horrible crime. When he looked around, he couldn't find any evidence. The clouds had turned grey and fused into a continuous mass over the land. His mother was napping and his father was napping and he was walking in his tennis shoes across the soggy earth. The weeds with yellow flowers and the tan scrub and the purple. No thought was a necessary thought and no action was required. There had been herds of hairy animals and there had been scalpings and outlaws and spacemen with bubbles to breathe in and lasers and wind. It was all a vast ghost on the plains.

* * *

On Monday Wade's teacher, Mrs. Avery, introduced a new woman to the class. The folks in the capital don't think Mrs. Avery knows how to talk about feelings, Mrs. Avery told them. The new woman arranged them in a circle on the floor around her. My name is Brenda, she said. She was large and maternal, wearing soft, nurturing clothes. I'm here today to talk with you about some scary ideas and feelings, she said.

Their hands popped up, and the children offered anecdotes of dead dogs, dead grandmas, dead fish, cows, neighbors, people in movies, baby brothers born dead, dead mothers and fathers.

My sister was stomped on, said a girl named LeAnn.

My daddy got took out, said a boy named Terry. The windows of the classroom were so dirty that the sky out there seemed smudged and colorless, grimy and webbed. Death didn't seem to Wade like a far-away place. The idea that before he was born he hadn't *been*, frightened him more. Fragments of children's stories drifted into his mind. The screaming children, the bloodstains by the monkey bars, the strange man in sunglasses. Some girl was talking about her auntie in heaven, but Brenda steered the conversation away from religious ideas. Brenda wanted them to talk about their feelings. It seemed that nobody had ever before asked such a thing from these particular children. Brenda had cards that showed frowning faces, smiling faces, each face tagged *happy* or *sad* or *silly* or *scared*. This seemed ridiculous to Wade. He decided to feel different ways, that didn't match those words, and not to give those feelings names. Later, Brenda stood in the center of the circle and wept. She wept for her sense of safety, for her dead friends. The children began sobbing around her.

* * *

Brenda took Wade aside to the book corner. She was concerned that he hadn't been sharing, and Wade thought that meant she was upset that he hadn't cried like the rest.

Maybe you could share some of your feelings just with *me*, she said.

Okay, said Wade.

She asked him what he remembered about that day. Wade concentrated.

I was right next to that girl, he said.

That girl had been shrieking and looking at the tattered remains of her arm. The blood just kept coming.

The teacher came out with some wet paper towels, he told Brenda. And he tried to soak up the blood, but he couldn't soak it all up.

You must have been very scared, said Brenda.

The man was shooting and shooting, said Wade.

He thought about his decision not to name feelings. Unfortunately, other people's feelings were too interesting to ignore. Since he didn't know how to discuss feelings without naming them, he decided to pair traditional words in unusual ways.

The man looked happy and frustrated, he said.

Brenda nodded.

He looked like he wanted somebody to play with, Wade added.

Do you think that's why he was so mad? asked Brenda. You think he wanted somebody to play with him?

He was mad and he was silly, Wade offered. Brenda looked puzzled.

He was sad and he was excited, he said instead.

It sounds like that man was very confused, said Brenda, but Wade knew she was really saying that *he* was confused.

Mrs. Avery interrupted them.

Miss Dinkins? she said.

Brenda, please, said Brenda.

She whispered to Brenda. Wade knew that she hated him, but Brenda was just annoyed by the less cheerful woman.

What are you getting at? said Brenda.

Wade heard the word "sick," and then something else. Mrs. Avery shrugged and returned to the circle. Brenda gave Wade a hard smile and patted his shoulder and left him there.

He remembered it all so clearly; that bloody, screaming little girl and the man at the fence. Somebody get her a Band Aid! Wade had yelled. At Circle, Barry was saying that he was inside at recess, doing his homework when the shooting began. Wade picked up a book about dogs on bicycles and looked at the pictures. Barry was saying he had missed the whole thing, crouched in safety under his desk, as they'd been taught to do in case of tornado. He had never been in danger; he had never seen a thing. Although Wade had seen Barry's picture in the paper, bawling and splattered with the dead teacher's blood, he accepted this new version as equally true. Nobody challenged Barry. Another child raised her hand, and then another child began to weep.

* * *

When the wounded children returned to school, there was a huge celebration. Cookies with frosting, and a march around the playground. Shortly thereafter came a whole range of tests. The other children had to draw pictures of the houses in which they lived. They had to draw pictures of their happy time; they drew pictures of swimming and snowball fights, throwing things at cars, buying new things at the store, wrestling with dogs, and blowing up the school. They were asked whether they would rather work under someone who was always kind or someone who was always fair. Wade was left to read animal books in the reading corner by himself. *The cheetah leaps through the air with all four legs bunched underneath and its supple backbone arched like a bow pulled taut.* He read about coyotes and hyenas and elephants made sad by their impending extinction. There were fewer every day. Wade discovered a word for what had happened on the playground. The children had been culled.

Shortly thereafter, a new line was formed at lunchtime. This meant that Wade had to sit by himself even longer, while other boys with bag lunches waited for their pill.

The days were getting hot. The boys especially had become less interesting. They didn't seem to have moods anymore, or even a mood.

* * *

Many years later, on the radio, a man was listing symptoms. You aren't sure who you really are, he said, or you don't feel like yourself.

If enough of the symptoms suited you, it meant you were a candidate for some new syndrome. A feeling of loss that has no referent, the man continued. The need to be invisible, perfect, or perfectly bad. High risk taking or the inability to take risks. The feeling of carrying an awful secret, the urge to tell, feeling oneself to be unreal and everyone else real, or vice versa. Lost memories, or blacking out a period of years . . .

Wade felt that way sometimes. It seemed he'd been to some colleges. He'd learned things and had brief affairs with the men who kept up the grounds. But he could remember it all if he really wanted to.

The man driving the car pulled over at a rest stop. I need to check my e-mail, he explained.

Wade wasn't sure how that was possible. The man sat at a picnic table and typed away at his laptop. They were somewhere in the desert, in transit from one dubious location to another. Their relationship was based on an accidental convergence of two paths of least resistance. They were both too lazy to try and change other people to suit their own preferences. Wade wandered off into the scrub. A dry gully twisted around through it and he could see how high the stream had been by the garbage that was stuck along the banks. Plastics and fast food cups and a surprising number of articles of clothing, shirts and rags and underwear, and bloodstained jeans. The desert was the worst place to hide evidence, because nothing decayed.

The land just went on. He was pretty sure there'd been human sacrifices around here, he could sense it. Blood had soaked into it. Blood was curdling and the sun was blazing. You couldn't see the creatures, but they were out there, waiting and chewing each other for sure. They sucked up each other's juices, he guessed. He walked haphazardly along the gully for some time, letting the heat and his thirst empty his mind. When he came to a barbed wire fence, he turned back. At the rest stop, the man was clicking his mouse and talking to him as if he'd been there next to him the whole time.

It really facilitates community, he was saying.

Wade guessed he was talking about the World Wide Web. This man thought everyone in the world together was turning into the planet's brain. It had become the source of a mild, but nearly constant irritation between them.

Not everyone has a computer, Wade said.

The man snorted.

I talk to people in Kenya, he said.

The man's skin was dry, hair frazzled and bleached. He seemed crisped, a little bit fried around the edges, like an asteroid that had come through the atmosphere a few times too many. Wade knew that his time with this man was approaching its end. The sun was blazing out here and the electronic screen seemed grotesque. Wade thought there must be a club of dictators or child murderers he was connecting with in Kenya. The man was wearing a stained undershirt and suit pants.

More evidence. Guilty, thought Wade, but surely nobody cared. He thought then that his mood was the same as America's, or he thought that his mood was exactly "America." The man shivered in the heat, as if he was finally ready to move on, but then he continued clicking away, a sort of hopeless scratching noise under the sun. There was a weird hair or blue fiber there where the shirt, drenched with sweat, was sticking to the man's back.

Stephen Beachy is the author of two novels, *The Whistling Song* (Norton) and *Distortion* (Harrington Park), and the twin novellas *Some Phantom/No Time Flat* (Three Roads Press). His writing has appeared widely and was included in *Best Gay American Fiction*. He teaches at the University of San Francisco.

Colette DeDonato

I am the person who is always asking too many questions. Some days I work like a private detective and others like a pirate. When I write poetry, I try to let my unconscious mind guide me, trusting that it will lead me to the places of urgency, the places where truth and meaning intersect for me. I have a daughter who is just learning to speak, so much of my work has been about being preverbal and finding our way into language. I have an obsessive mind, so writing allows me to explore things I think too much about: poetry, political structures, and what are known as the five poisons in Buddhism—greed, hatred, ignorance, pride and craving. Writing keeps me engaged with the world.

As a WritersCorps teacher in the late '90s, I worked with youth in transition: runaway and homeless youth, soon-to-be-incarcerated youth, and with young girls in an after-school program. I came to WritersCorps fresh out of a M.F.A. program—with postmodern narrative structures and poetics (theories!) still swirling in my head. I'd been doing social work while in school and had felt split between what I viewed as the privileged academic world of creative writing and the gritty reality of people I worked with who did not have enough education to get a decent job or enough money to feed their children. I wanted to find a real world application for poetry.

WritersCorps seemed like the place where these two worlds could converge. Teaching homeless youth for the first two years changed my own relationship to writing. At first it made me dubious. Who cares about poetry in the mid-'90s? What could I share with these kids that would be at all helpful? The kids I worked with were operating on their more basic needs: Will I end up on the streets or in jail? What will I become if I drop out of school? My writing workshops offered respite, a chance to let go for an hour and see what was inside your head, or a chance to dive a little deeper into the muck and come out understanding it a little better. We read a lot of poems in that class. I felt like each one of those poems was a gift. It was helping them to be better readers—and better observers.

At some point I realized that teaching made me believe in my own writing again. I stopped analyzing "my place" so much and realized that there was a great joy that came out of writing. The joy was mine and it was theirs. I was thrilled to be passing that on to these kids, and I was recharged with belief in the way in which writing opens the world up to us all.

Winter

A man came to me,

distilled and angry from those four letter words
falling somewhere between the cushions of comprehension.

He was real and bruised like one
who has loved long enough.

His knees bent, his eyes closed,

I took him through winter and all the quiet possessiveness of
   routine.

He said it was the doing and undoing of all thought.

So what I said, I wasn't looking for knowledge.

There are too many things to understand.

Only in the early morning hours, dark,
when the headsmith's shoes are left outside the door,
leaving us to run barefoot over our parallel lives,

do we narrow down enough to be.

Purview

We hallucinated our gods.
We drove our Western stakes into the ground.
Pretend you haven't noticed. Pretend
the revolution.

Think of how the sun feels resting
on the end of your nose, nothing
to complain about.

But you,
always complaining.
You, in the garden
making holy pavement.

This Is That

You have been told not to run with scissors in your hand, but you are an iconoclast and a well-dressed one at that. Hence, the privilege of being pantheistic. The benefactors have all set sail in another direction. Nothing promised to you is a relief anymore. Of course, this too is conjecture. But there are no villains in this story. There is no embargo, no accidental castration. Nothing is foolproof or visibly charitable. The superintendent is unkempt and defiant and the visionary is beguiled, squeezing avocados in the market. Surely someone is suing the surgeon and the virtuosos have resigned themselves to austerity, despite the terrible cliché. This is just how some days go, completely absent of your cogent input. Congratulations! The Buddhists say don't resist. The overeaters say give your self over to the eleventh hour. The dogcatchers say freedom has it limits. The dog says when in doubt run fast. The Italians say join us for dinner. The president says let me codify the truth until you don't recognize it anymore. You see, there is something useful about inspiration. You are free to ululate now, and move about the earth.

Colette DeDonato is the editor of *City of One: Young Writers Speak to the World* (Aunt Lute Books). She earned an M.F.A. in poetry from San Francisco State University and lives in Santa Cruz with her husband Carlos and their four-year-old daughter Lucia. She is currently working on a collection of essays, one of which appeared recently in the *New York Times*.

Ryan Grim

Before I approached the middle school where I was going to teach on my first day, I could hear it: the screams of 300 children filled the air for blocks around. As the four-story brick building in Northeast Washington, D.C. came into view, I could see hands and heads hanging out the windows. Several weeks into my after-school program, though, the principal said that my program would have to be terminated.

The reason?

It interfered with the federally funded after-school program that was instructing children on how to pass the standardized tests mandated by the No Child Left Behind legislation. All other after-school programs had been canceled already to make way for the test preparations. The message was clear: In the new world of standardized tests and top-down directives, poetry had no place—not even after school.

For some of my students, poetry was a respite. For others, it was a way to reconnect to the school system, giving them hope about an effort that otherwise seemed futile. The students and I didn't take the cancellation lying down. We took it sitting down—in the hallway outside the locked library—and we continued to write poetry. The library was locked because the school couldn't afford a librarian. Probably nothing in those books would teach the kids how to pass the standardized tests anyway.

The principal wasn't really against the poetry program. Poetry cuts across lines of ideology—think fascist Ezra Pound and leftist Walt Whitman. But the principal feared for her job and for her school's funding. She told me that if her school didn't continue to improve its test scores, she would be partially blamed for allowing a program to continue that competed with the after-school test-taking class. That was a risk she was unwilling to take. But I'm glad it's one that WritersCorps continued to take. Poetry is an oasis of freedom available to prisoners of all stripes, whether it's the state, poverty or depression holding the jailer's keys. I am proud of my work as an accomplice.

the calm before

I leaned back
stretched my legs

on the grassy hill
and watched from afar
as the clear sky melted
around us.
Lying there
I was the world
the stars in sky
the river below
the grass in my shoes
the hair on your neck
and the glass on the sidewalk.
I was everything and I was nothing
while a few hundred yards off
some kids were drinking beer
outdoors
and the police were on their way.

they own the block

the kids outside are working the corner
again still dressed head to toe in blue
blue hat on top of blue bandana blue
jacket covering their giants or lions jersey
I can't tell which giants would make more
sense the home team but not much does
and they're not much of a home team all
the way in new jersey last night a truck
blew by so loud I swore it was in my bed
room set off car alarms with its engine
they own the block says so on our building

Ryan Grim covers Congress for politico.com. His work has appeared in *Rolling Stone, Harper's, Mother Jones* and *Salon*, and he is a regular contributor to *Slate* magazine. A former writer with the *Washington City Paper*, he won the 2007 AltWeekly Award for best long-form news story. He is writing a book on the history of American drug culture, due out in June 2009.

Joy Jones

I am happiest when I chronicle what's common-place, celebrate the ordinary. I find the plain and simple situations of life to be the most fascinating and the most profound. I love to write in all genres: fiction, non-fiction, poetry, plays, articles and for children. My love of the written and spoken word comes from my parents: Daddy who used to make up bedtime stories and Mommy who introduced me to the joys of the library. When I write, speak or perform, I hope to give the audience that same sense of magic and revelation that I experience when I am touched by words. I have known since childhood that I was a writer. After all, a writer is simply one who writes. By that definition, a first grader drawing his ABCs would be considered a writer. However, I wanted to know where I stood among professional writers and if my writing delivered any import or impact. Did I have a gift? Did my words affect others the way others' words affected me?

WritersCorps gave me the opportunity to pose that question and then live its answer. Yes, I was a writer who could paint pictures, provide information, occasionally amuse or inspire. But more importantly, I became a vehicle to allow others to discover the power of their own words. I taught in a variety of locations in Washington, D.C.—Kramer Middle School, Backus Middle School, Turkey Thicket Recreation Center and at St. Elizabeths Hospital, where I led writing workshops with mentally ill patients. One emotionally troubled teen at the recreation center told me that when he told his therapist how much he liked the poetry classes, writing poetry became part of his treatment plan. The act of teaching writing pulls me off of my high literary horse. Working with children in particular is a study in mirrors. There's always a student who I identify closely with, but the child who gets on my nerves often turns out to be a person who reflects several of my own character flaws.

Rx

Are you tired,
run down, depressed and blue?
Have a headache,
a backache, a heartache or two?

I have just the prescription for you:
take two poems and call me in the morning.

Write a book, beat a drum, rap a rhyme.
What?
You tell me
you have no talent, no magic, no skill?
I tell you
if you don't dance every day something is wrong with you.
Paint pictures as if your very life depends on it—
it does!
An artist can change
lemons into lemonade
gators into gatorade
an escape into an escapade
by practicing senseless beauty and random acts of kindness.

Do you feel bad?
It's because you haven't had your creative daily requirement.
Are you sick?
Well, you should be—
a lack of art causes constipation and mental illness.
Don't call no doctor,
buy a box of crayons.
Didn't you know that playing a musical instrument
raises your IQ by ten points.
Poetry cures cancer
and a song sung through your tears
will do more to draw God nearer
than a hundred Hail Marys.

Sing nappy-headed songs,
play polka-dotted, kente cloth-colored riffs.
Write tunes about the late fee on your rent,
the bus ride home,
the lady at work with the arched eyebrows,
the hair on your big toe.
Don't think it foolish—
millions have been made by people
who sang songs about

chestnuts roasting on an open fire, little green apples, funky stuff
    and big behinds.
(Chances are you even bought one.)
Be mad and original and comic and thoughtful and
glorious in your play
for it will make you wise and mystical.
See if you can get your next orgasm by writing a poem.

You are made in the image of your Creator
so you have no choice but to be Creative.
Anything less is a sin.

Joy Jones is the author of *Between Black Women: Listening With the Third Ear*; the acclaimed children's book *Tambourine Moon* (seen on *The Bernie Mac Show*); and *Private Lessons: A Book of Meditations for Teachers*. Her plays have been performed in New York, California and Washington, D.C., and she is the director of the performance poetry ensemble The Spoken Word.

Katherine LeRoy

The power of poetry has enabled me to cross cultures, and WritersCorps was instrumental in opening up a variety of these cross-cultural opportunities in my life. My assignment as a member of the first WritersCorps cadre in 1994 was at Hospitality House, a drop-in shelter for homeless and runaway teenagers. It was a culture that was far removed from any other population I had ever worked with before. Poetry was a bridge between our cultures.

Poetry allowed me to enter into an environment of distrust, fear and pain and make connections with an amazing group of young people over the two years I worked there. Through creative writing workshops and one-on-one mentorships, I was able to build trust and create an atmosphere of safety and healing. I saw these young people use the written word to help them in their struggle for clarity and stewardship over their own identity. Within their community, they became wonderfully creative artists whose words had the power to inspire others.

WritersCorps prepared me for the work I then took on in schools and community centers throughout Asia. In Thailand and Vietnam, my husband and I trained teachers and community leaders in the use of the creative arts to inspire and unite the populations they worked with. We formed the company Steakfish International in order to bridge cultures through creativity. As an expat living abroad, I gained an acute understanding of what it feels like to be different: culturally, physically and most especially linguistically. With poetry, I can create bonds that transcend rules of grammar and engage people on a fundamental level. This connection is what continues to inform my work as an educator and an artist.

Erosion

Written just before leaving Asia in 2002 after two years of living and working in Lampang, Thailand.

this won't be the way it really happened.
not the bone or the blood
because biology is shifted
with the wind.

a sleight of hand,
time whines a siren song
and pales memory,
renders it oddly shaped and unmanageable.
a week, a month,
two years of your life.
what does it fit into?

leaves on a tin roof
or the clack of plastic dishes being stacked
or even the way the old women catch your eye
then look away.
this won't be the way
it really happened
because that is both expired and unborn.
a pokerfaced demon with soft white wings
dancing circles at your feet,
raising a riddle of dust.

but primitive instinct still bewitches us blind.
the vapors and odd ghosts
lift us up from our geography,
and no longer earthbound
we rubberneck
our imperfectly charmed lives.
carnage and celebration,
reaching for the grammar,
this will be an approximation.
something lived
yet merely remembered,
in a language of checks and balance.
measuring the grooves in your skin,
at the corners of your smiling.

count the scars,
the odd bumps and bruises,
the way your back bows
more than before, a slight stoop.
and your sandaled feet,
now brown and calloused.

how does this measure
against dusk-light and pure cloud?
the way teak breathes
its own history,
like a bonfire or a small river.

the way expectation rubs up
against experience,
wearing it thin and soft
at the edges.
an erosion.

this will be lopsided and jagged edged.
it will be crudely stated.
and with a sliver of vision,
it just might bleed.

Katherine LeRoy brings over fifteen years of experience to her work in cross-cultural and arts education. She has taught in various settings throughout the San Francisco Bay Area as well as abroad, most recently in Thailand and Vietnam, where she was an active member of the Hanoi International Theater Society. She is a founding director of SteakFish International, which partners with schools, nonprofits and community-based organizations in providing cross-cultural and English language workshops.

Birthright

Uchechi Kalu

I began teaching with WritersCorps when the world around me felt like it was collapsing. Within the span of a few months, I lost my youngest brother to a car accident, my older brother was deported back to our native Nigeria, my writing mentor June Jordan was dying of cancer, and the September 11th tragedy left the world in a state of collective grief. I needed to make sense of the chaos, and most of my students at International Studies Academy in San Francisco were trying to do the same. Some of them were trying to survive in a new country, and others were trying to survive their adolescence without ending up dead or in jail. They came from Yemen, El Salvador, the Philippines, Haiti, and the various neighborhoods of San Francisco. I worked with native and non-native English speakers whose stories left me inspired, angry and humble. For some of these students, poetry was a subject in which they could shine because it allowed for minimal language with maximal impact.

I wasn't that different from many of the students, and once I shared this with them they allowed themselves to trust me. I grew up across two countries, three states and the chaos of a brilliant but violent father. He loved language and often gave out assignments that included reciting biblical scriptures and preparing for school spelling bees. Like many of my students, I went to school with stories that I didn't know how to tell, and with a desire to escape my father's brutal hands. I knew what it felt like to miss school for INS appointments and to wonder why my educated parents worked at McDonald's for so many years. I knew what it felt like to have police show up at the door with news that one of my brothers was either dead or in jail. I write poems filled with rage, love, anger, beauty, and most of all, hope. Over the years my subjects have changed, but my purpose remains the same: To tell the truth even if it is painful, and to find beauty and possibility in unimaginable places. I don't separate my need to teach from my need to write and perform. Each informs the other and plays a role in the transformative process.

I also write as a catalyst for personal and social change. I believe silence only engenders shame. As June Jordan said, "To tell the truth is to become beautiful, to begin to love yourself, value yourself. And that's political, in its most profound way." When those young people stepped on stage and read their poems, everyone in the room understood them more than before. The teachers, parents and other students jumped up in celebration. Young men who described themselves as too "hard" to write poetry sometimes stuttered or cried while reading poems about the friends and brothers they had buried. When we can articulate those things that are so close to our hearts, we are able to allow others to share their stories, and we no longer feel alone in our grief.

What Happened to the American Dream?
for my parents

this is for my father
who threw a newspaper
in my face and said
study all the words
you don't know
someday they'll have to listen
to an African girl

the son of a village chief
who only knew the sound of a growling belly
the man trying to make something
out of the ordinary

the man with the proud heart
that took him overseas
but left him unable to say sorry or please
to his wife and children

and no one told me
about grief
and no one told me
about anger
about blame
about the shame of what went on
the hushed voices
the violence

no one told me about sorrow
about burying baby brothers
and wondering if this was part
of the American Dream equation

the fascination with success
but no one at the Embassy
said anything
about depression
and war after war
and an unending recession

no one said anything about Black Pride
coming in an eight ounce bottle
of hair relaxer
that is
if you want
the brothers to look your way
or if you don't care
you can just stay single
for the rest of your life

what about fast food
making four dollars an hour
what about working three jobs
and trying to hold your head high

no one said your teenagers
would want
to wear thongs and nominate Eminem
as their national hero

no one said
you would feel like a fool
after you locked your son's room
and tried to keep him home at night
but he seemed to sneak out the window
using only a broom
and no one told you
you would fume
and become your father
my grandfather
staring into the beautiful eyes
of your child

no one told you
and if they had

would you have washed your hands
clean
of it all
said no to tight jeans and strip malls
and suburban lawns
'cause you couldn't
guarantee all your children
would win the national spelling bee

would you trade the lipstick and belly rings
for a one-way ticket
home
so at night you could sleep
without your heart beating
fast enough to keep you awake
wondering why your children
couldn't just be Nigerian
in America

would you ask God
for your son back
if you packed your things
and said goodbye
to the American dream

would you remember
you told me
never give up
would you remember
you flipped
burgers and burned fingers
so you could pay the rent

would you remember
how you swallowed the boss's
nigger this and *nigger that*
and kept your face straight
even when he spit on your new
pair of shoes
did you choose to leave
or did you fight
work late night shifts

knowing one day
you would walk back into that restaurant
order lunch
and remind the same man
to add Dr. to your name
when addressing you

do you wonder where the dream went

do I disappoint you
having spent my college days
studying words and rhymes
and meter
and trying to defy silence

but the American Dream theme
you see on TV
doesn't come with
an infomercial
that reminds you
this American Dream
was brought to you by
dark hands always bending over
underneath a scorching sun
or women lying on their backs
attacked by soldiers or husbands

no one told you
this dream was sponsored by
the yellow hands
who stitched these three-piece suits
or the janitor stooping for trash
after the fans have left the stadium
so the rent won't be late again

what about every story
sitting in the throat
afraid to be put back
on a boat or plane
if these words spill out

what about never making the mortgage

no matter how hard you try
or how much processed food you flip or fry

no one told you
you'd have the ability to smile
after you've been to Auschwitz
Sabra and Shatila
Phnom Pen
Rwanda
Lebanon
Syria
Liberia
Nigeria
even if your teeth look
like they've been washed in urine
and are crumbling like the war torn
capital city of your country

no one told you
you could still
laugh
tilt your head back
and know your eyes have seen
whole people
marched to death
and somehow you didn't make it
to that line
or roll call
that morning

even if your back is sore
from too many days pinned to the floor
a soldier's body
permanently pressed to your thighs
it's your imagination drifting
to better days
and the promise of a shower
to wash the blood from your legs

that laugh
the confirmation of breath
the declaration of a heart beat

the certainty of finding joy again
the determination to make one breath into millions
the realization that hope can defeat death
the blessing of rain on parched earth

and don't get me wrong
this is not about forgetting the past
I'm here to tell you
I've lived with anger until it ate my insides
like a bottle of aspirin
I've lived with sadness
soaked myself in it
until I couldn't pick myself up from the floor
I've put my feet in shame's shoes
until I couldn't walk anymore
and my blisters were the size of dimes
I've lost track of time because guilt
has been my favorite pastime
I've carried other people's pointing fingers
on my back
survived the attack of glares and stares
and jeers from my very own parents
who just wanted me to enjoy the Dream
I've let off steam
blamed everyone from my mother and father
to my breasts and thighs
I've stared into the night
cursing the moon
for letting the world turn upside down
I've swooned over would be lovers
who've fought this same battle
and lost to the bottle
broken into pieces all over the sidewalk
and I've gone running into the night naked
feet bleeding from all that glass
and all the fear
not wanting to relapse
into the past

and this is for anyone
who knows this story all too well

for anyone whose given up
on the American Dream
for anyone whose tired of looking mean
and throwing darts at anyone
coming
your way
for anyone whose life
didn't turn out
like you planned
for anyone feeling damned or cursed
for the truth teller spitting his first verse
for the boxing gloves you never picked up
for the boxing gloves you need to set down
for starting over
for beginning again
for beginning again
for daring to dream
one more time

Uchechi Kalu was born in Abia State, Nigeria in 1978 and grew up in Missouri and Texas. She is the author of *Flowers Blooming Against a Bruised Gray Sky* (Whit Press), which was nominated for a Northern California Book Award in 2007. She studied poetry with June Jordan's Poetry for the People at U.C. Berkeley before teaching in the San Francisco WritersCorps. She lives in Brooklyn, New York.

Will Power

For me it all revolves around the story. What is the story historically? What's happening in our cultures, in our communities? What was disastrous? What was beneficial, heroic or complex? The storyteller is a bridge, from society's past through the present, on to the future. So how may we in the present hear ancient stories, connect them to the issues of today, and then re-interpret and modernize them so that the ancient wisdom of days gone by lives and breathes for the folks that come after we're gone? Most of my creative work up until this point wrestles with these types of questions.

With my show *Flow*, the question was how do we use the stories of our ancestors, and our neighborhoods as guides to "flow" through life. In *The Seven*—my adaptation of the Greek tragedy *Seven Against Thebes*—I'm asking the other side of that question, how do we shed the baggage of our ancestors? The past isn't always a glorious past.

When I'm going into a community to work with youth or college students, I teach them the skills and tools and craft of storytelling—the basics, and other innovative techniques that I've developed through hip-hop theater—but I also push them to question the relationship between their present, past and future. And both in my teaching and in my art, I try to get people out of the dichotomy of "good" and "bad." Good storytelling and good social engagement go beyond that dichotomy into more complex relationships. I try to write plays that paint characters in full dimensions in order to work toward the full truth of a community and its stories. And I hope we move more toward that in our world as well.

I joined WritersCorps in San Francisco during its second year, in 1995. It was a job, but it wasn't a job, because it was something I loved to do. And it was the last official job I had before becoming a full-time artist. WritersCorps was a great transition in helping me make that leap. I remember the camaraderie of the artists, of the writing teachers coming together, excited about the work we were doing. I worked in the Filmore, the Western Addition of San Francisco, teaching storytelling and poetry, and the work helped me to sharpen the tools I needed to engage the community. WritersCorps helped set me on the path that I still follow.

From *Flow: A One Man Show*

CHARACTERS: *New Ground, Man with Bloody Hands, Woman, Bus Driver*

NEW GROUND:
Baba-dee-da-dabeydoo-dee-da
Baba-dee-da-dabeydoo-dee-da
Baba-dee-da-dabeydoo-dee-da

Well I had my headphones
Jay-Z was playing
You know Jay Z?
Yeah the guy, big pimpin' Jigga? yeah right
So, I had my head phones, Jay-Z was playing
I was walkin' down the street listening to what he's saying
Something about, about "getting' paid"
It don't mean nothin' cause they just brought down the World Trade

Then I came across a man
He was in a zone
His
Hands were all bloody he was punching a stone
Say he wanna do something wanna do it soon

I said ya probably oughtta get some healin' for those wounds
He say

MAN WITH BLOODY HANDS:
Let's kill all the arabs man

NEW GROUND:
He say

MAN WITH BLOODY HANDS:
All the motherfuckin' arabs man

NEW GROUND:
He say

MAN WITH BLOODY HANDS:
Or at least get em out this land

NEW GROUND:
He say

MAN WITH BLOODY HANDS:
Every American must take a stand

NEW GROUND:
I say

I don't recall making your folks pay
When the building got blown by that man McVeigh

Plus your people aren't native in this here land bro
If somebody kicked you out, now where would you go?

Baba-dee-da-dabeydoo-dee-da
Baba-dee-da-dabeydoo-dee-da
Baba-dee-da-dabeydoo-dee-da

I was visiting the south going from state to state
And since I was in the south Mrs. Jackson was on play

You know Mrs. Jackson? Mrs. Jackson
The song by Outkast
Sorry Mrs. Jackson—whooo—I am for real?

So anyway
From Alabama and Kentucky I had seen
I thought I would go next down to New Orleans
So I hopped on a bus, and I started to roll
Through towns where the people used to be bought and sold
Those folks worked in the heat and even the cold
Then fought Jim Crow let the story be told—so
On the Greyhound it's so cold—hey what up? What up?
Cause the bus driver had the air condition way up
Then a woman with a child in her arms and one on her knee
In broken english she says to the driver

WOMAN:
Too cold—please

NEW GROUND:
And the driver just ignored her kind of shrugs it off
He said

BUS DRIVER:
Shoot I like the cold, it keep my Jerri-curl soft

NEW GROUND:
Now the child that's on the women's knee is starting to cough
And sneeze . . .
So the woman asked the driver again

WOMAN:
Too cold, sir, help!
And the driver stopped the bus he said

BUS DRIVER:
Ok that's it!
I'm tired of you Mexicans always askin' for shit
Now this is my buss! Tired a' you people!

NEW GROUND:
I say, but sir, didn't your ancestors die so that you could be equal?
He say

BUS DRIVER:
Why don't half a ya'll mind ya business? Hmmph.

NEW GROUND:
I say . . .
Nothing

Will Power's critically acclaimed one-man show *Flow* and his off-Broadway production, *The Seven*, have forged a new style of theatrical communication. He has been interviewed for television by Carson Daly and Bill Moyers and has appeared on HBO's *Def Poetry Jam*. He starred in the film *Drylongso* and was featured in the documentary *All Fathers Are Sons*. Power has received the Peter Zeisler Memorial Award, the Jury Award at HBO's U.S. Comedy Arts Festival and the Trailblazer Award from The National Black Theater Network.

© Tara DeMarco

Jime Salcedo-Malo

My father was born in the rancho La Yerba Buena, in Mascota, Jalisco, and migrated north to the border town of Mexicali as a youth, came into age, and like many, went coyote bound north for Los Angeles, where I was born. Years later I would join him in continuing that northern journey up the Califas coast, eventually ending up in San Francisco where the story continues.

This story of migration runs deep within the lives and consciousness of Latino Americanos. Those of us who were born suns/daughters of immigration know the cultural schizophrenia of growing up between two cultures, two worlds, between two languages, two distinct existences—living and growing up somewhere in between. The manifestation of Chicanismo and Spanglish is living proof of how far from our parents' Mexicanismo we often travel to find that place of belonging . . . identity . . . of change . . . home.

Many Chicanos are rooted in the ideas of community, but struggle with the contradictions of a Mexican culture rooted in collective traditions, and an acquired culture of individualism—the feelings of aloneness that some carry deep within our hearts. Our lives are complex. Although some of us will never struggle financially and physically the way our parents did, we still face the struggle of finding ourselves and a connection within a society whose customs and norms are at times contradictory to those of our parents, our families and ourselves. Writing has helped with this process. It has been my road map.

I had the opportunity to teach creative writing and performance art with WritersCorps for four years. I was able to witness souls unfold before me. I read stories before they were printed; I helped preserve them so that they would not be forgotten. In the process, I learned to let my own story unfold, to give it form so that I grew along with the students that I worked with. Without a doubt, this was a privileged position to have.

In 2005, I left WritersCorps and the Bay Area to transition from teaching creative writing to pursuing my doctoral degree in clinical-community psychology. I learned so much from my students in those four years with WritersCorps, and I have carried these experiences with me into my graduate studies, as they have informed and helped shape my future as a clinician.

167

Mexico Series

I.

El De-Efe

La ciudad de Mexico
Ciudad antigua
Tratando con toda
Su historia antepasada
Pasar como sociedad
Moderna del oeste,
Pintándose el pelo de rubio
y cubriendo sus arrugas
Con cultura pop del

USA,
Coca Cola,
y Sony DVD.

No mames guey,

Es algo de una curiosidad.

II.

Fifth Direction

We
plant olive
trees to replace
each uprooted
Mexicano dream
left behind
on some dirt road
in Norte bound coyote rides.

sin titulo

I.

en la plaza de
        mascota, jalisco,
el lunes pasa
        sin sentirse,
el aire libre,
        calmado,
sentado,
esperando a
        un primo,
y los pájaros
        cantan,
acompañando la banda
que toca
        la de un puño de tierra,
mientras los carros pasan
                en ruta a su destinación,
sin prisa.

II.

pronto llega la noche
con su sensualidad sabrosa,
aire puro, helando rostros,
el clima, fresquesito,
cachetitos chatos,
como la primera estrella de esmeralda,
alumbra calles empedradas,
y los viejitos sentados en el kiosko,
cuentan cuentos folklóricos,
nuestra sangre corre,
entre sierras de jalisco
tapatías,
las venas que llueven oro,
y cuerdas de guitarrón,
mi rancho, mariachi, tequila y son.

tierra mi tierra,
orgullo,
y estas mujeres,
son las más hermosas,
las de mi patria,
mi patria tapatía y no me rajo jalisco,

aquí no pertenezco a los de abajo,
soy mexico con un poco de americano,
pero más american que mexicano.

III.

estrella al norte me da un pestañaso,
me asegura que fue mi destino
estar aquí
sentado en este banco
en este momento
en la plaza de mascota,
por cierto.

Jime Salcedo-Malo has performed his poetry in the U.S., India and Mexico, and has recorded two spoken word CDs. His chapbook *Walking Stories of Migrations North* was published by poetrytelevision.com. He taught writing, spoken word and "self determination" with the San Francisco WritersCorps from 2001 to 2005 and is now a doctoral candidate in clinical-community psychology at the University of La Verne in Southern California.

© Sara Press

Judith Tannenbaum

When I was a little girl I listened to my father's stories, to my aunts' and to the stories my older cousins invented to scare me. My great-aunt told me about her childhood in Russia, my mother read me stories from books. As a teenager I wrote stories on paper; as a young woman I began writing poems and continued doing so my whole adult life. From the beginning, as listener and then as creator, I loved words and that state of diving, as one of my former San Quentin students named the process: aligning one's self, going deep, letting the words flow to the surface and out of the pen to the page.

For almost four decades, I have shared poetry with men and women in prison, with young kids in primary schools, teenagers in continuation high schools, as well as retirees in community college classes. My work as a teaching artist has allowed me to share my own love for poetry, and to put into practice my vision of art as an activity that belongs to all of us, an activity that is a human birthright. And all the while I have kept writing—poems, mostly, and prose about teaching and about prison, including *Disguised as a Poem: My Years Teaching Poetry at San Quentin.*

I joined the San Francisco WritersCorps in 1994 as a mentor teacher/teacher trainer, and I have remained ever since. I love the opportunity to offer what I've experienced and learned from my own practice to the next generation of teaching artists, an offering that is its own kind of story-telling.

From the novel *Day's Light Beginning to Deepen*
Chapter One: *Not Yet*

"The child's foot is not yet aware it's a foot,/and wants to be a butterfly or an apple," Pablo Neruda wrote in the 1950s. Not yet: we begin with Neruda's not yet. We begin in the womb, one cell into two, a foot not yet a foot, tremendous becoming. Before there's a boy with red hair and a love for wet puppies, before there's a girl with black curls. Before Spirit narrows to Story.

We begin with Life in the uterine lining. Four weeks: a mouth, a pointed tail. Eight weeks: a heart that has been beating for close to one month. Eleven weeks: lighter than the weight of a letter. A shoulder, an elbow, eyes sealed and shut.

Nourished in the womb of a happy or sad, particular, woman. Maybe this woman rubs her belly as she stands at her kitchen's white sink. Maybe she sits on the back stairs, smoking a cigarette, staring into the night. A man, a woman, a city. A garage apartment, a marbled mansion, a crumbling cottage nearby the sea. A grandfather with the love of good books, an aunt with a mathematical mind. Generations of blue eyes and healthy lungs. A susceptibility to nervous system distress. Bunions at thirty, glasses at forty, freckles that turn to moles in old age. Ancestors bearing the weight of history with ululation and song.

A time, and a place. These babies, still in their mothers' wombs on the last New Year's Eve of the 1940s, will soon be themselves: Rachel Rosen, Sarah Lustig, Lia Bayes, Barbara Dale. They will be four of the global 2.5 billion, four of the 3 million born in their own country that year. For their whole lives, these girls will be called *Baby Boomers*, a post-war blessing to a world in which 50 million had been recently killed.

These girls will be born into a land of blue Melmac, dinette chairs in gray vinyl, stainless steel napkin dispensers, and aluminum trim around Formica-topped tables. A land of Hershey's chocolate and Hires Root Beer, Suzy Parker in the magazines, and Nat King Cole over the airwaves. A land where automobiles bear names rich and exotic: *Riviera, Bel-Air, Catalina*. A land of red Texaco stars.

Names on most everyone's tongue: Ralph Bunche, Douglas MacArthur, Althea Gibson, Alger Hiss, Florence Chadwick, Judy Holliday, John Wayne.

Nineteen fifty will be the year of the McCarran Act, UNRWA and the Kefauver Committee. In that year, President Harry Truman will send troops into South Korea, and approve the production of the Hydrogen bomb. The Chinese will march into Tibet; Ho Chi Minh will fight the French in Vietnam. That February, Joe McCarthy will speak to the Women's Republican Club in Wheeling, West Virginia. He will wave what is actually his own laundry list, while claiming the sheet documents 205 Communists working in the State Department.

In 1950, *The Los Angeles Times* will advise its readers to report anyone protesting the Korean War. "Get his name and address and phone the FBI," *The Times* will exhort.

That year, 15 percent of the University of California faculty will be discharged for not signing a Non-Communist Affirmation Pledge.

That year, listed in the Report of Communist Infiltration in Radio and TV will be: Leonard Bernstein, Lee J. Cobb, Gypsy Rose Lee, Burgess Meredith, Arthur Miller, Zero Mostel, Orson Wells and Pete Seeger.

George Bernard Shaw will die in 1950, as will George Orwell, Nijinksy, and Charles Richard Drew, the African American physician who developed modern blood banks, but who withdrew as head of the program in protest over the American Red Cross's racial segregation of blood.

A quart of milk will cost twenty-one cents, a loaf of bread fourteen cents. Minimum wage will be seventy-five cents/hour. The average weekly salary for an industry worker: $60.53. Black and white TV will offer *The Lone Ranger, Your Show of Shows, Philco TV Playhouse, Hopalong Cassidy, Your Hit Parade* and *The Howdy Doody Show.*

Langston Hughes's *Simple Speaks His Mind* will be published in 1950, along with Thor Heyerdahl's *Kon-Tiki, The Family Moskat* by Isaac Bashevis Singer, *The Lonely Crowd* by David Riesman, and Immanuel Velikovsky's *Worlds in Collision.* Gwendolyn Brooks will win the Pulitzer Prize in Literature in 1950, the first Negro—the word of the era— woman to do so. Gil Hodges of the Brooklyn Dodgers will hit four home runs in one game that baseball season.

Our four girls will be born into a world of chiffon and organdy. Dungarees will be worn with ballet slippers, velveteen ball gowns with little jackets. Orlon will be invented in 1950, and the year will see also the first appearance of Miss Clairol hair dye, Smoky the Bear, Minute Rice, and Xerox copies. The first self-service elevator will be installed by Otis Elevators in Dallas; Diners Club will issue the first plastic credit card. Babies born in the United States in 1950 will play with Slinkys, Cooties, Lincoln Logs, Tinker Toys, View Masters, Duncan yo-yos, Crayola crayons and Fisher-Price Buzzy Bees.

Not yet, but that very year, the births of Henry Louis Gates Jr., Gary Larson, Jay Leno, Jane Pauley, John Sayles, Cybill Shepherd, Stevie Wonder. And Rachel Rosen, Sarah Lustig, Lia Bayes, Barbara Dale.

Not yet, not quite yet. In this last moment remaining, please remember the possibility of *butterfly,* of *apple.* Please remember the billions walking the earth, beings who will never meet in the market or stand in the same post office line. Millions of women who will remain strangers, though they all rock their babies to sleep in the night. Cupped hands the world over scooping grain. Ringed fingers, hennaed palms, knuckles raw from winter's dry cold. Each pair of lungs breathes in and out. Body next to body on the subway's long seat, intimate as a slight smell of sweat, a brush of soft coat sleeves. Intimate, and unknown. Each life one thread; each thread woven with others; fabric so vast, no human eye can hold the whole.

Judith Tannenbaum is the author of the memoir *Disguisged as a Poem: My Years Teaching Poetry at San Quentin* (Northeastern University Press), *Teeth, Wiggly as Earthquakes: Writing Poetry in the Primary Grades* (Stenhouse Publishers) and a two-person memoir written with Spoon Jackson called *By Heart: A Prison Conversation* (New Village Press, forthcoming in 2010). She has published several collections of poetry and has served as training coordinator for the San Francisco WritersCorps since 1998. Judith also edited two books for WritersCorps: *Solid Ground* (Aunt Lute Books) and *Jump Write In!* (Jossey Bass).

© Sean Evans

Kathy Evans

WritersCorps got me out of the suburbs. I was in the inaugural WritersCorps, the San Francisco 1994-95 group, and Clinton had just been elected president. He had pledged money and energy to revive AmeriCorps, and WritersCorps was one of its tributaries. There were about twenty of us from all over the United States, diverse in age, background and skin color. I crossed the bridge four times a week to teach in the inner city, a world apart from the one I had come from, the world of Volvos, little league baseball and pressure for high SAT scores. My first assignment was in San Francisco's Tenderloin District, where I worked in a center for community resources and development, teaching immigrant children poetry, which was a way of also helping them to learn first-time computer skills. I loved those kids, the ones who lived in small apartments, sometimes ten to a family—or no family at all—some with very limited English, others, wise beyond their years because of what they had witnessed on the streets. One student, Alan Nyguen, had no concept of what poetry was or meant. Every time I mentioned "poetry," he thought I was talking about a "Poet-Tree." One day he typed this poem:

> **POET TREE**
> Today I went to the park.
> I saw a tree.
> I like the tree.
> It's a different tree.
> It spells words.
> One day it grew my name.
> Birds come on it.
> I always come to that tree.

I just loved the little poem. It was selected not only for the first WritersCorps anthology, *Flavors of the City*, but also was made into a giant poster and placed all over San Francisco inside the fancy new kiosks that decked the city streets. Alan was about seven years old— I'm sure Alan was not his Vietnamese name—and had moved to San Francisco from outside of Saigon. He was so proud of the poem that he carried it around in a small window in his wallet next to the family pictures.

A few months after the WritersCorps assignment had ended, while I was working at a routine office job down on Folsom Street for a consultant firm, Alan's mother tracked me down and asked through an interpreter over the phone if she could come to the office. She showed up at the office at noon—Alan a step behind her—with dishes and dishes of home-cooked Vietnamese food. She wanted to say thank you from her heart, her hands and her kitchen for the poem. I told her that Alan wrote the poem, that there was no need to thank me. Nevertheless, her generosity was not forgotten.

Juvenile Hall

Today in Juvy Marcel says
He's gonna' sing his poem,
that two weeks ago he didn't even know
what a poem was,
that it just came out;
it just came out of him, he says
like a baby comes out of a woman,
that's what he says,
as if he knows.
He says he'd never even written a poem before,
but this one just wants to be sung,
and he smiles crooked-like, looks
charmingly cockeyed,
places his arms on the classroom podium.
"Now, I know you're gonna' want to laugh
when I sing my poem
and I'll just ask you brothers to wait,
to hold your laugh until I'm done,
I'm just sayin' wait."
And the big boys at the back
in their faded orange t-shirts and dark sweats,
with their shaved heads and sneers, some with
cheek scars from a quick knife, or pierced lips—
the boys from Richmond, from the hood,
some with biceps that seemed bolted on,
they just stared at Marcel,
watched him close his eyes like a skinny choir boy,

fill his lungs and sing
about his girl who had the baby anyway,
and his baby girl,
how she just came out like a poem—
that sweet baby girl, how they'd made it
together, then lost it;
sang until the brothers in the back
wanted to sing too.
Seriously, joined in at the end.
I swear the whole class up at Juvy was stunned
when Marcel was done with his poem—
the guards by the door, the boys at the back,
the parole officer in blue,
the nurse who dispenses pale pills in Dixie cups,
and the poetry teacher, who was all of a sudden
just one of them, one
with them, one with Marcel
and the brothers up in Juvy
because sometimes a poem
just wants to be sung.

Quatrains For The Sophomores

I tell the students writing is a moment of awareness.
Just go from the outer world
to the inner world. Start here with the
green of spring

and the blossoms going wild
along Sir Francis Drake Boulevard.
But we are inside, and I don't mean the inner world.
I mean, we are inside the portables.

And we are as hot and sticky as cotton candy
at the fair—a new form of trailer trash,
sitting at fake wood tables,
in plastic chairs with metal legs.

beige walls pocked with thumb tack holes
and one lonely poster of Steinbeck. We're aliens.
Some of the students put on their head phones,
others looks around, distracted

by what's truly in bud, the girl in the pink tube top,
by the crows cawing outside the window. But some
of the students, surprisingly, stay focused like good
little monks trying to save civilization.

A small-framed pubescent boy has his head down
on the table resting it near her braceleted arm—
An apple between them.
This is the last hour in heat and spring,

the last period of the day, and I don't blame them for
slumping over like primates. I love the Sophomores at
any cost, their minds inside their own myths, cell
phones, instant messages—

the blonde in green, the boy in the corner with hair
that looks almost yanked right out of the scalp,
drumming on the table top with # 2 Dixon pencils.
He must be a drummer in a group called Flunked.

Hello. Out there, I say, You Hoo? This is Captain
Poetry. This is an air raid. Everyone drop to the
floor like Keats. Get under your desks. Put your
hands over you heads. Something is about to blow.

Kathy Evans is the author of three collections of poetry: *Imagination Comes to Breakfast, As The Heart Is Held* and *Hunger and Sorrow* (winner of the 2005 Small Press Poetry Prize). Her poems have appeared in journals such as *The Atlantic Review, The Southern Review, Yellow Silk* and *Americas Review*.

John Rodriguez

© Jenn Ross

I'm Puerto Rico by blood, Harlem by birth, Bronx by geographic responsibility and male by nature, but I'm a writer because I wrote myself into existence. Words were there for me when I was discovering who I was and what I could do and be. It was an option I never thought about until I happened upon some writing by other New York Ricans, which was an education I received outside of formal schooling.

I tried to facilitate that same kind of "outside learning" in my own poetry classes with the predominantly brown and black teenagers of the Bronx. My WritersCorps students learned how to read between lines for contextual understanding and incorporated those same techniques of deconstructing verse to construct verses of their own, reflective of their thoughts, feelings and circumstances; however, the critical consciousness and the freedom to express original identity that they developed were outlawed in their schools. The result: although my poetic education alongside them opened doors for me, my students were systematically pushed to drop out of high school.

My mission now as a Ph.D. candidate is to document our class' poetics/dynamics as an auto-ethnographic thesis, one in which a single entity's voice (written, published, amplified) resonates with the struggle and authority of a people.

The Last B-Boy

I hate these kids, B.
They can spin on one
finger for five years
and not have a trago
of style. Or charisma.

So I take em to Bx River
with a wild Indian step in
my toprock waiting
for the break. DJ does the jigga
jigga and I hear my anthem:
"Apache." Original text

conga and guitar music
that your father used
to listen to. It tells me
to be fast. Fourteen again.

/ I go down / do footwork
both ways / head to floor / leg
up / freeze (I smile / then) sweep /
into swipes / and it's cleaner than that
new sneaker smell / and it's faster
than the cash register at Dr. Jay's
I feel like a new pair of Adidas
with a matching Kangol
suede striped and sheen / and the beat /

The beat is getting to me
The beat is getting me to
weigh the arguments I promised
my wife about the power moves
She said:

> *Ba-bee, you know I love you*
> *and to me you'll always be*
> *number one but you know these*
> *kids these days. They breakdance*
> *like John Woo is filming them.*
> *You told me you need two aspirins*
> *and a massage just to watch.*

I promised myself
back in '78 when I was getting
cuts on my shoulders from the
schoolyard backspins back when
the dance asked me the question

> *How good* are *you?*

I swore to myself to always
give the same response

I am better than the last b-boy

/ so I push my luck
I power move, I flare:
once, once and a half, twice /

only I don't feel
so good no more.
One wrist reminds me of
all the years I've gained.
The other the weight.
My elbow drops like vocals
before the break
I fold / I fall / I fuck up

/ automatic stomach crunch
knees to shoulders tight, close
and pop and / coindrop
and drop and drop and drop /

I hear oooohs and aaaahs like
I meant to do that

> *What you think all
> the practice was for, kid?*

/ continuously backspinning smooth
and easy / I see my homies'
hands in the air but the spots are coming
into the corners of my eyes
and the crowd sounds
like my alarm clock telling me to
wake up and go to work

/ one more freeze
head hand shoulder
off floor legs figure four / sneaker
grab / freeze (I hurt / then) / cee-
cee / sweep / stand / spin /

Before taking my
place in the circle
I throw up the old school
double peace signs.
One for the last b-boy.
One for the next.

John Rodriguez worked with WritersCorp from 1997 to 2000 at various community-based organizations including The Bronx Writer's Center, Mind-Builders Creative Arts Center, Bronx Residential Center School and Women's Housing and Economic Development Corporation. His poems have appeared in *Bum Rush the Page: A Def Poetry Jam, Home Girls Make Some Noise!: Hip-Hop Feminism, Hokum: An Anthology of African American Humor, Rattapallax* and elsewhere. He is working on his Ph.D. in English composition and rhetoric at the CUNY Grad Center.

Seshat Yonshea Walker

Anytime you reveal a place or an emotion on the page, it's therapeutic—and allowing others to read or see these emotions is always an inner battle. In the past, writing was my voice, as I was so shy and introverted. Writing for me is a way to be witness for yourself, to heal, to move on, to remember and let go. My writing uses the "unpopular" voices to describe familiar experiences and vice versa. My first production, *Black Gurl*, was a collaborative piece exploring the childhood experiences of five black women.

A natural born activist, I come from backwoods, pigs' feet and outhouses. As a songwriter and playwright, I try to convey the complex in the simplest of ways. I like to relate to people's experiences by using my own. I'm an artist. A wife. A mother. A country bumpkin. Forever a black gurl. A band nerd. A brownie. A protest marcher and an observer. Like any of my writing, music is another way I can communicate and further evaluate. I don't like music that is too high-brow, nor music that insults people's intelligence. I believe there is such a thing as thought-provoking music you can dance to. Poetry and plays are no different.

I was motivated and inspired each day I worked with the students at Lincoln Middle School and McFarland Middle School as a D.C. WritersCorps instructor. I was motivated by their perspective and creativity even on days when they would challenge me.

From the play *Black Gurl*
middle of the road

(in this scene, seshat recalls a scary childhood moment when her favorite aunt took her on a trip to the middle of the road. seshat tells the story in a five-year old voice and her adult voice. despite how dangerous the situation was, seshat's five-year old's natural innocence, imagination and love for her aunt kept her somewhat oblivious and less fearful.)

little gurl: These people keep messing up my parade
        don't they see my aunt cissy is the bandleader
        and i'm twirling my flag
        that's okay cuz i can be an acrobat

i can walk high on my tightrope
so they can't touch me
mommy always says i got good posture

big gurl: aunt cissy's husky behind is my guide
my five year old hands palm each buttock
teetering on either side of the road
balancing my life on a never-ending yellow beam

lg: ease on down, ease on down the road
i don't know why the police made us stop
they should make them people stop cursing at us
it don't matter cuz when they leave, we start
our parade again
don't my aunt cissy's face look like a marshmellow
my mommy says her medicine blows it up like that
sometimes when mommy's not looking
aunt cissy lets me poke her cheeks (laughs)

bg: i don't remember how we got there
only the town police stopped us
aunt cissy's puffy face silent
my mother says her medication
makes it swell up that way
the police warn us to keep to the sidewalk
but somehow we always ended up back
on that golden line

lg: we left mommy at the red apple
she was getting my bubblegum ice cream
but aunt cissy says we're going to make
better ice cream at grandmom annie's house
and we stir it in a washing machine

bg: aunt cissy tells them we're going to grandmom
annie's, but i tug her corduroys to remind her
we ain't got our skirts on
she pets my nappy head and i follow anyway
even crossing that chester bridge

lg: i don't like the bridge it's too shakey
plus when i close my eyes i still hear

that boy crying in the river
i tell him his mommy ain't looking for
him no more
he says my mommy is looking for me

bg: as we cross the bridge's 200-year-old
rickety body, anxious river below,
i squint my eyes and secure my fingers
into my aunt's back pockets
wondering if that boy's body will float
to the top
the second one to drown during fireworks

my aunt cissy whips around
throws me a high-pitched *don't look down*
i see why I'm her favorite
our button noses / slanty eyes matching

lg: i think i see mommy
her glasses are gone
her face is sticky
i think she ate my bubblegum ice cream
and she got my school picture
it's sticky too
i tell her it's okay she ate my ice cream
cuz we can go to grandmom annie's
and make even better ice cream
but mommy says we got to go cuz it's
suppertime
so we get into the brown hornet
that's what the kids on the bus call
mommy's car

bg: i don't remember when they found us
just that mommy ain't have her glasses on
when she squeezed me
and i could taste her salty tears as she
kissed me
our legs intertwined dangled half in,
half out her dookey brown mustang
aunt cissy sits quietly in the backseat
her babyface swollen even more

      she stares out the grimy back window
      down the road

lg: mommy turns around and gives aunt cissy
      four yellow pills and a pepsi
      i tell her maybe her face will blow up
      so big this time, she can float down to
      grandmom annie's house
      if she does i hope she makes me some
      ice cream

Seshat Yonshea Walker is a songwriter and playwright living and working in Washington D.C. One of her original songs will be heard on the debut album of Tamara Wellons (Ocha Records). Her second multimedia staged production, *Will She Love Me When I'm 64?*, will debut in 2009. Walker has consulted for such events as Brave New Voices International Poetry Festival, AfroPunk, Central Park Summerstage and The Black Luv Festival.

Livia Kent

When I started working for WritersCorps I wanted to teach my students about form, meter, slant rhymes, line breaks. Instead, they re-taught me about the freedom that comes simply from trusting in the power of language. As they explored emotions and experiences through the safety of metaphors, they shared their work with one another in class and with the larger community at readings and slams. Watching their confidence grow, I became inspired to start tearing the cloaks off my own writing, to risk stripping it down to its most vulnerable state. Every time I picked up my pen, I imaged my students hanging on my shoulders, ready in their scrutinizing teenaged way to call me out for any inauthentic move I might try to make on the page. It was a fertile time for all of us.

At the end of my first year at Sousa Middle School, a seventh-grade boy who hadn't spoken or written more than two words all semester raised his hand to share his response to a writing exercise inspired by Neruda's *Book of Questions*. "But Steve," I whispered, glancing at his paper, "you've only written one line." He shrugged. The title of his poem was one of many prompts I had offered, one I doubted any of my students would attempt to tackle. "What is Eternity?" he read. "An abandoned house that is never vacant, a black smudge that is always clean." The class gasped and broke into applause. Afterwards, several of his most disparaging peers would admit that Steve's words were precisely what they'd sought in answer to the question "Who am I?"

Mother Tongues

A Memoir

I.

My mother converses with spirits and tells me about it, casually, as if they were old friends she'd run into in the tampon aisle of the drugstore.

I fainted once in the tampon aisle of the drugstore, and in the brief black before hitting the ground, I thought I heard spirit voices too.

It turns out those voices belonged to two women who had been shopping nearby when I went down—and I went down, I later learned, because you're not supposed to stop taking antidepressants cold turkey.

You're supposed to gradually decrease the dosage, even though you decide one day that you don't need those yellow pills, that without them the world is fine, you are fine, life is fine.

How was school? my mother used to ask.
Fine.
And your test?
Fine.

She would always press for details, but *fine* was all I could let loose. *Fine* was everything and nothing, truth and fiction.

All my life I've known this:

Before my mother knew she was pregnant with me a voice stopped her at the top of the stairs: *It's a girl and her name is Livia.*

When I tell this story I actually do the voice. I make it deep and heavy, then I open my arms and end by saying, *Lo and behold.* Usually,

no one believes me.

II.

Crete, 1994. A high school year abroad.

In Greece, we are assigned new names. In Greece, they call me Erofili—Erotic Love Friend, loosely translated. Menelaus, the red-bearded king of *The Iliad*, has red hair and a red goatee and lives in the room next to mine.

I put on a jacket from the year my field hockey team won the State Championship and go outside in the garden to smoke. I taint the body my mother gave, and the name—embroidered in black cursive on my chest— unravels a bit. *Livia*, I say out loud, but those five letters sound as far away as my mother is in America.

I call her the next morning. I call to hear her say my name. I call to say, *The Samarian Gorge, we're going tomorrow.* I am smoking a cigarette, exhaling softly so she won't hear.

She has been to the Gorge before and starts to tell me it's full of spirits when a stranger peeks into my phone booth.

Mom asks, *What was that?*
Some guy wants to borrow my lighter, I gloat. I am fifteen. I am autonomous. I understand Greek.

And, after a moment, I understand the silence on the other end of the line.

There is silence too in the Samarian Gorge. I hear no spirits, only an occasional hawk overhead screeching into the wind.

III.

Livia will go to China.

She was walking in a parking lot, stepping over rainbow slicks of oil when the voices told her this. I was three at the time. A year later, with me in tow, my parents crammed twenty-six suitcases full of *necessities* and boarded a plane for Beijing where my mother would teach English.

I had hair so blonde it looked white in certain lights. This was 1980; China had only recently opened its borders to foreign travelers. I learned Mandarin in a few months and don't remember a word of it now, but my mother has cassettes of my little-girl voice babbling away in all the right inflections.

She says I am reciting nursery rhymes I learned in my Chinese school, ones I sang as my father pedaled me to and from class in a bamboo seat mounted on the handlebars of his bicycle.

While the other students sat straight-backed, hands folded atop their desks, I sat on the teacher's lap as she painted small red circles on my pudgy cheeks.

I can see the word *spoiled* scroll through people's minds when they learn that I'm an only child. The air becomes bloated with uncomfortable pictures of ponies and ribbons; and I think of China, of the way my mother insists that at any given moment a hundred hands were clamoring to rub my hair, my arms, my marshmallow legs.

When I returned to the States I went straight to summer camp and demanded that my counselors carry me up the mountain we were meant to hike that day.

IV.

While I was at camp, my parents stayed at a B&B, in a room that once belonged to the writer Edith Wharton. One night while my father slept, my mother wrote me a letter.

I hope camp is going well. I hope you're eating well. I hope you're enjoying yourself. I hope . . . And then, as my mother tells it, her pen began to write on its own: *Livia, Livia, Livia.*

My mother addressed the musk in the air. *Edith? Is that you?*

Yes, the pen wrote, wobbling a little on its inky point.

She would go on to tell my mother that someday I would write a book about the wilderness.

Twelve years later, in college, I wrote the words *nest* and *knobby* and *node* but could only envision the oak of a dark bedpost, the way my then-boyfriend had his hand around it when I opened the door to find him naked with another girl who actually smiled at me while I stood there.

Nests unraveled. Trees grew top-heavy and suddenly fell over. The world became loose and ashy, and I was powerless to wash it off. So I stopped bathing. I stopped eating. My teeth grew thick sweaters of plaque, and I didn't care enough to find my toothbrush in the mess of clothes on my dormroom floor. I was miserable and malnourished, and the one time I tried making my way to class, I fainted in front of the Student Union.

The Health Center called my mother. She flew out the same day. I remember leaning on her tiny frame as she took me to see Dr.

Wyatt, a thin-lipped wiry psychiatrist who sent me away in less than twenty minutes with a prescription for antidepressants.

The pills were solid, bright, and yellow in my hand, but I buried them deep behind my tongue, drowned them in water, sometimes vodka; and they offered little by way of solace. I remained flat and spindly, except for those ephemeral times when I managed to slither into the skin of some character in a book. My appetite for books was insatiable.

I found Edith Wharton's *House of Mirth* at a basement sale and gingerly parted the pages, but Ms. Wharton sought to communicate through my mother alone, who was on a plane to London somewhere over the Atlantic Ocean when the voice came back.

Livia will marry by twenty-one, drop out of college, get pregnant, and move to Paris.

After I graduated and turned twenty-two my mother told me what the voice had said. *I waited to see if it would happen,* she added, *and it didn't.*

V.

What did happen is I went traveling.

I went to places my mother had never been—except Paris. I avoided Paris. I avoided getting pregnant too, though I had sex with several men and fainted twice while traveling in India (but that was from dysentery) and once in Australia (but that was because I was hungover and dehydrated).

By the time I left Mexico I felt I had strewn the malaise of growing up, like breadcrumbs, across the terrain of eight different countries. Four states and five apartments later, I find myself living twenty minutes from my mother's house.

Last night we strolled together in silence past the alley where I once built a snow fort with the best friend I haven't heard from in sixteen years; past the driveway where I used to rollerskate until an old man accused me of trespassing; past the tree where I had my first kiss that I know lasted thirteen seconds because my friends voiced the countdown; past the pool where I cracked my head on the diving board, won first place in a swim meet, and lusted after a lifeguard who had a fancy way of blowing warnings on his whistle. We even walked past the woods where as teenagers my friends and I drank beer and smoked pot from hollowed-out fruit that was easily ditched when the cops appeared.

Did you hear anything? my mother asked when we had come full circle and returned to the house.

No. No spirits. But I did hear her breathing. I tried to match her inhalations, her taking in of the world. I felt how she held me deep inside her body, beyond the walls of her lungs and the boundaries of her brain. I felt the space between mother and daughter cease to exist in that brief moment before the letting go, the exhalation that always comes and returns us to ourselves.

When the phone rings later, it will be my mother.

Mom, how are you?
Fine, she'll say.

But I'll know that she is tired, that a pinched vertebrae keeps her up at night, that she has just finished the dinner dishes and will probably watch a documentary on PBS.

Livia?

I'll wait for the name to form itself around me, a silky cocoon of invisible threads. I'll wait for the knots to tighten, for the ends that remain undone to fall away. I'll wait for the room to smell milky, like the cream my mother insists tightens the skin around her eyes. I'll wait to feel firm, and then I'll answer.

Yes?

Livia Kent taught for the D.C. WritersCorps for five years. She holds an M.F.A. in creative writing from American University where she received the Myra Sklarew Award for Outstanding Novel. She is currently a deputy director at Heldref Publications and continues to lead writing workshops throughout the Washington, D.C. area.

© Kenley Neufeld

Leslie Davis

For me, writing poetry is a plunging deep into my own personal alchemy. Turning my lead into gold. Writing is a way to bring together the sacred and the ordinary, and a way to examine all the spaces in between. What we find there is fascinating, scary and nourishing. I like to shine a light on places that we don't yet know or haven't allowed to emerge.

In WritersCorps, I taught at Newcomer High School where newly arrived immigrants spend a year or two studying English before moving into the San Francisco public school system. Working with these young people from all over the world was a cultural opening that I eagerly embraced. Conducting a creative writing class with teenagers speaking up to ten different languages taught me a lot about the universal power of language. This stretched my ability to integrate non-language elements such as visual arts, music and video into my teaching in a way I never had before. The richness of their cultures, languages and hormones ended up in their poems as they found their voices and tested the waters of a new land and its language.

Go as a river

Wear it well my friend   this
Is my power color   superstar
Drive home into   cotton fields
Almond trees in pink bloom

Everyone fighting   my body
        grain mill   white egret in the
Pasture   another freight train

Water our sweat pea   give
Lunar blood back to the earth
Crop duster   tell me
What my palm says   domesticity
        didn't work for me in that city

Had to go   tilt the wrist
Watch fledglings test their new wings

I hear you woodpecker

Remember to use these   names
Of towns I drive through
Selma   Ceres   Salida
Catch the baby   I never lose
Things he claims but I see things
Differently   another casual barbeque
Spring has us in its clear blue sky
There's a cistern down there
What can I catch in mine   rain
    water dreams ghosts

Tonight at dusk the birds
    finally
Singing so loud almost
Violent with joy

My sensitivity

The empress showed herself to me
Full-bellied and ripe
Placing the three jewels upon her
Swollen womb   we
Remain alert and realize
I like things that mean things

Somewhere along the line I
Reconnected with my divinity
8 of swords reminds me to
Dig into misperceptions   voices

You little wonder
You hidden ability

A bringing forth a   cluster
I am collecting my gold

Leslie Davis is the author of *Lucky Pup* (Skanky Possum Press), and her poems have been published in *damn the caesars, Skanky Possum, In the Grove* and elsewhere. She lives in Ojai, California with her family.

Milta Ortiz

I write because I have to, out of a basic need to stay sane. As a little girl, I discovered journal writing as a way to deal with my bi-cultural reality, having moved from El Salvador at the age of eight. I knew things were different for me, and that it went beyond the language barrier. I knew enough English to get by—yet not enough to understand the customs, the sense of humor, the overwhelming liberties we have in this county. As a girl it was too complex for me to grasp, so my diary became my best friend, and I began to shape an identity for myself on paper. When I learned that my mother's uncle in El Salvador was murdered for sharing political ideas that were in opposition to the government, I would never again take lightly my ability to formulate a critical opinion. The first story I wrote came out with the fury of a whirlwind, and I titled it "Speak Your Mind."

There aren't many Latinas writing today, not at the slams, not in creative writing departments, not in the literary world. This urgency motivates me to keep writing and performing. I can't tell you how many young women thank me for reaching out to them, for speaking their stories, their disappointments, their hopes. I've been blessed with the power of words, and I speak loudly for my grandmother, my cousins, all the women who for some reason or other don't have the option of writing. For me it is about reclaiming our myths, harnessing their power, and asserting our birthright to take up space in the world.

Writing is a vehicle for finding self, freeing self, and building community. I have so much joy to give, because I do what I love and remain true to myself. So in my teaching with WritersCorps, I urge my students to trust in their inner voice. In all, I learn from them as much as they learn from me, and they leave me feeling inspired and grateful.

Always In Between

my mind burns like a country in civil war

while Paris Hilton and Niki Rich
hit 50 K in a shopping spree
the Colon is overthrown
by American green

a family in El Salvador struggles
to eat beans
        and tortillas
making meals with what's left

                I sling
Shirley Temples for two-fifty apiece
hope my customers drink
enough martinis   to leave me
a 20% tip
for my college degree

my mind breathes like a country in civil war

half consumer, half visionary
my heart pumps the echoes of FMLN
Farabundo Marti Liberacion Nacional
modern day robin hoods
                descendents of Che

my mind breaks like a country in civil war

thirteen years of primo against primo
cousin killing cousin in El Salvador
then ten years more

the country kneels to mass production
today's sermon—PROGRESS—
factories and malls anchor in
and the dollar reigns
but most Salvadorians only window shop

sometimes it feels like I'm on a bridge
all I want to do is stop
but I have to keep going
70 miles per hour

so I sing to myself
the Our Father in a soulful melody
I'm not even Catholic anymore
but I pray

in English and Spanish
how Mami taught me

I'm a Loroco flower
uprooted and replanted
in star-spangled soil

I'm American and Salvadorean
both and neither
      my purgatory on this bridge

it takes all I am
to withstand
the fog
of this place

Milta Ortiz is one third of Las Manas Tres, an all women spoken word troupe, and a member of La Peña's Hybrid Experimental Performance Ensemble. She holds a B.A. in creative writing from San Francisco State University, and her poetry has been published in *Coyolxuahqui, Cipatli* and Propergandamag.com. She wrote, produced and performs *Scatter My Red Underwear*, a hybrid play. She teaches for WritersCorps at Mission High School in the Mission District of San Francisco.

The Shapes of Listening

© Matthew David Powell

Ellis Avery

I spent my WritersCorps year (1995-1996) at the Lavender Youth Recreation and Information Center (LYRIC), a networking and advocacy organization for gay, lesbian, bisexual, transgendered and questioning people aged 23 and under in San Francisco. In my after-school creative writing class, we collectively created a radio show, each student writing from the point of view of one of the characters: a planeload of drag queens downed in rural Maine, and the small-town residents into whose lives and beds they messily crashed.

Crackton, Maine, our radio show, was a riot, and made everyone feel safer, both as writers and with each other, about taking on more sensitive material—the closet, their parents, sex and love. Writing allowed them both to sharpen the tools that would ensure their triumphant survival—glamour, illusion, wit and style—and to articulate their private truths.

As a teacher at Columbia University, thanks in part to my experience at LYRIC, I work not only to help students be the best individual writers they can be, but also to write in community, to hunger for each others' work. Teaching is draining, but writing is lonely. Writing in community gathers us around the proverbial campfire and reminds us why we do this: because hearing stories helps us make sense of the world. Because telling them helps us make sense of ourselves.

From the novel *The Teahouse Fire*

The first paragraph opens the book; the rest of the excerpt falls two chapters in.

1866

When I was nine, in Kyoto, I changed my fate. I walked into the shrine through the red arch and struck the bell. I clapped twice. I bowed twice. I whispered to the foreign goddess, and bowed again. And then I heard the shouts and the fire. What I asked for? *Any life but this one.*

* * *

The fire was a loud animal. It sucked the breath out of me. I groped and staggered, *forward, away,* through the screams and the groaning buildings. Men called for water to save their homes. A child's voice wailed, *Mother, Mother!* and no woman answered. When a horsedrawn cart pushed past me, I thought, *I could have climbed up on that.* I was sure I had missed my chance, but then one of the horses spooked, shrieking on its hind legs, and the driver beat him about the head with wet rags to stop the falling sparks. I reached for my St. Claire medal and ran toward the horses. I shimmied into the cart, flattened myself against a load of silk. When we had cleared the smoke and the fleeing crowd, I scrambled out again and ran, ran into the dark.

I ran, and then I walked, unseeing. My lungs felt charred. Occasional breaths of incense burst through my sobs, so I must have passed shrines. I walked and walked until my breath sanded my throat. I was so thirsty. Beyond a dainty bamboo fence, I saw a place ahead where the moon shone wetly. I climbed the fence: no water. I passed a stone wrapped in string—a boundary marker, I learned later—and saw beyond it a rough stone pillar. Its smooth worn top formed a cup, holding water. Oh. I leaned into it and drank like an animal. When I wiped my mouth, mucous clung to my wrist from crying.

I was in a garden of moss and stone. I saw a tiny wooden house with a square hole in the side, like a door for a baby. A rough stone formed a step in front of the square entrance; I climbed up on it and looked inside. "Hello?" Nothing. I crawled in. I felt woven straw under my hands, a Japanese floor, so I untied my boots and kicked them behind me into the stone garden.

So this is how, smelling of fire, snot drying on my face, I first came to the teahouse Baishian. I lay flat on the floor and slept.

When I sat up in the dark, the fire felt small and remote to me, like a story of a girl in a fire. I was real. This house was real, all silvery wood and moonlight: the most beautiful place I had ever seen.

The room stood small and bare, with no furniture, two pale *tatami* rectangles with a wide dark polished floorboard between them. In the heart of the room, I saw a gap in the floorboard, a perfectly square hole, like the door I had crawled through, but smaller. The moon peeped in through scattered windows, turned the straw floor white, made the floorboard gleam, but left a perfect square of night untouched at the center. It frightened me; I looked away. In the corner beside me, a tiny step up from the *tatami* floor, I saw an alcove, three feet wide by some two feet deep. The brightest splash of moon fell on the alcove floor:

a beautiful piece of wood, brown-black, with a thread of white running across it like vein of bright marble. The room was a mirror for the moon. It seemed to hold its breath.

All it lacked was its fairytale inhabitant, the spirit princess for whom the little hole I had crawled through was a wide gate, for whom seven feet by six was palace enough. Maybe she lived deep under the earth, and wafted in like smoke through the dark square in the floor. Would she be warm enough in here? I lay down, cold, and drew my knees to my chin.

Someone was walking outside. It was strange to hear a footstep here without the wooden clop of sandals, but I was not mistaken: *shff, shff, shff,* as if walking barefoot, a light, knowing step, quick. The walker paused, as if startled, outside the house where I lay. A female voice whispered a word in Japanese: *Older Brother?*

I heard a long pause. And then a head appeared in the square doorway— I shut my eyes, breathed deep sleeping breaths. *A little foreigner,* said the voice.

I peeped again: the head was gone. A large object appeared in its place. I was afraid. It was dark, a creature, a stiff dead dog, and then I made it out. It was a Japanese pillow, a wooden box topped with a cloth pad. A thin cloth followed the pillow, and then I heard someone pick up my shoes, all in one resolute motion, and set them on the cloth inside the room. Then a back, a grown woman's back, appeared in the doorway, shoulders moving; she was peeling off a pair of socks. I saw her arm reach in and set them on the cloth with my shoes. And then the woman herself crawled in through the little door, straightened, and loomed over me. Scared, I closed my eyes again.

Koneko, she said under her breath. A word I knew, less endearing than it sounds in English. Cats and kittens are dirty in Japanese, and by definition, stray, only tolerated—like the ship cook's mouser— if they earn their keep.

And yet she paused over me, then crouched. I felt her face near mine. A damp feather of her hair touched my arm. I tried desperately not to change my breathing. Why didn't she scream at me?

And what kind of person, clearly not poor, went barefoot? I heard a slow, distant *tok, tok:* a night watchman pacing with his wooden clapper. I figured it out. The woman was hiding too. *Older Brother,* she'd first said: where was he?

I opened my eyes. A stark white face was looking straight at me, a monster with no eyebrows. I flinched. *Boo*, she said. A Japanese sound, *ba*. I cowered and froze up, gasping. I saw the mask ease into a faint smile, and I uncurled and simply stared at her, my heart loud in my throat. She stared at me too.

I saw a young woman, perhaps sixteen to my almost-ten, with long alert eyes, a narrow nose. A long face, longer for the lack of eyebrows, washed clean. She was like the moon, like the dark wood shot with light. Her long drying hair was a silk river. Her eyes were lights. I shivered, from the cold, and because she was so beautiful.

Her beautiful nostrils flared. Her beautiful face rippled with distaste. *Kusai*, she said. *You smell bad.* I hid my face in my hands, ashamed. She gave a tiny dry seed of a laugh, and turned away from me. I opened my eyes and watched her. She wore two robes, a dark one over a light one. She stood, as if dispensing with an interruption, and took off her outer robe. She lay down on her side, facing away, on the pale *tatami* between me and the hole in the floor, settling her pillow under her neck. She sighed, and again I heard a hint of laughter. And then she spread her kimono so that it covered us both.

My eyes felt bald, I opened them so wide, with shock, with gratitude. *Foreigner. Little cat. You smell bad.* Even my mother chased stray cats off the roof with a broom. She didn't spread her clothing over them to keep them warm.

My mother was dead in New York.

No. My mother was alive; she was safe and far from fever. A spirit princess, she had vanished down a square hole in the floor, under her bed, and left a false body behind. I touched my St. Claire medal. I couldn't think.

The woman's hair had touched my arm. The woman's hand, the back of her hand, had flickered across my side when she shook her robe smooth over us. Who had touched me, since I left home? Only Uncle Charles. I couldn't think about that either. The cotton of the woman's kimono lay across my cheek; it smelled of old incense, dark and sweet. I watched her breathe. Her narrow back was a tall ship lifting gently on the waves. She was the princess of the moon mirror. She was a bright vein in dark wood. I slept.

In the gray dawn, the woman sat beside me and pointed to her nose, the way Americans point to their hearts to talk about themselves. "You," she said. I am you? You are you?

She picked up my hand and took my index finger, they call it the person-pointing finger, and pointed it at my nose. "Me," I said, or maybe I didn't grasp the game, so I said, "You. Me. You. I don't understand. Aurelia?"

"U ra ya," she repeated.

"U ra ya," I agreed.

"Ura-ya," she said dubiously, as if I'd told her my name was Road Toll, or Wet Mop. Her face cleared, and she lifted my hand toward me again, gently. "Urako," she said softly, pleased with herself. *"Miss Urako."* So it was a name, then, a name stressed like Erica or Jericho. This morning it was mine.

"Urako," I repeated, and she smiled.

I was the last thing she'd imagined finding here, her face told me, as she stared at my dress, my knitted socks, my necklace. What had she come here for last night, barefoot and in secret? *"Older Brother?"* I asked, remembering.

She looked at me for a moment, then understood that I'd tried to say a Japanese word, then realized what I'd said. Her eyes widened soberly. She said something, and like her, I had to think about it for few seconds. *Dead.*

There was so much I hadn't learned, but I remembered a word from my grammar. *"Sad,"* I said.

"Sad," she repeated. She looked down and away.

To cheer her up, I touched my nose for her and said *Urako* again. Her face bloomed.

Ellis Avery is the author of *The Smoke Week,* a nonfiction account of life in Manhattan just after 9/11, and the novel *The Teahouse Fire,* winner of Lambda, Ohioana and Stonewall awards, which is being translated into seven languages. She lives in New York City and teaches creative writing at Columbia University.

Michelle Matz

In high school, when I began to deal with issues of sexuality, I began, in essence, to live two lives: my life of poetry, which was honest, and the rest of my life, which was a creation of complicated lies I told so nobody would know I was gay. It is the love of poetry as a medium in which one can be one's most authentic self that I have tried, in my eight years with WritersCorps, to show my students. I hoped that poetry could be for my students, teenage immigrants faced with the daunting challenge of writing poetry in their non-native language, what it was for me—a way to tell the truth. The truth of cramped third floor walk-ups, war torn countries, the taste of ripe mango. I loved my students, and I loved how poetry was our common ground, our shared language.

I've been writing since I was a kid. I remember when I was eight, maybe nine, I wrote a terribly trite and transparent story about a little girl whose father worked long hours. My grandmother, with whom I was very close, carried a copy of the story in her pocketbook for years. I used to love rummaging through her purse for a hard candy and seeing the story tucked away in the inside pocket. That was when I first started to see myself as a writer.

The Pear Tree

long after summer stumbled
into autumn, and autumn into loss,
the pear tree across the street
sagged fruit

days, I moved
through ordinary sounds:
emptying the dish rack,
the small music of a garbage can
pulled to the curb,
a knife slicing thin a loaf of bread

nights, that pear tree saved my life,
the way it gripped its rotting fruit,
refusing the hungry earth

Ars Poetica

After dinner, my mother stood at the sink
and washed dishes,

her back curved
like a stem towards light,

while I set up my paint-by-number kit
at the kitchen table:

a straight row of numbered colors,
a small bowl to rinse the brush.

My father told my mother
again and again

to let the dishes soak,
don't run the water.

I chose the picture I wanted,
a landscape with 34 colors,

while my mother let water pour from the faucet
like blood from a sudden wound.

I was careful to rinse the brush
between colors, not to turn yellow into fog,

red into bruise. The river stayed its course,
blue held blue, birds in flight soared

perfectly still.

Pieces

She is apologizing in pieces.
First, in late August

on a mosquito-thick night and now,
sitting across the kitchen table

her chair slightly turned away.
She is apologizing for death,

her imminent own, and I am distracted
by the sounds of the neighbor's six year old

twins sitting halfway up, halfway down
the back stairs counting to three:

one hand-in-hand with two, held-in breaths,
three dragging its heels behind two

in a moment suspended as one of the twins
reminds the other that it's better to do it

all at once, a second grader told him so. She
is apologizing for death, and I am distracted

by thoughts of popsicle-sticky fingers
prying a band-aid off a scabbed knee,

believing it will hurt less if they do it quickly.
She is dying in pieces, jagged-edged and slow-falling,

the way the sun goes down evenings without her. I want
to say *this cannot be happening, not to us* but it hasn't rained

in weeks and the screen door is broken and we didn't get around
to fixing it today and her coffee is already lukewarm and wasn't

it hot just a minute ago and so I say *listen to Allison's boys
they're trying to pull off a band-aid in the least hurtful way*

and I say *maybe they should just let it disintegrate
how long do you think that would take?* and pushing her chair

back from the table she says *forever.*

Michelle Matz taught for the San Francisco WritersCorps for eight years. She is the author of the poetry collection *Atilt* (Finishing Line Press) and recipient of an Individual Artist Grant from the San Francisco Arts Commission as well as the Mary Merritt Henry Prize for poetry at Mills College, where she received an M.F.A. in creative writing. She also holds a M.Ed. from Stanford and a B.A. in psychology from Wesleyan University.

© Michele Elliott

Michele Elliott

I am forever intrigued, shocked and surprised by the tragedy and beauty of being human. Being human, our legacy. Fully expressed in how we make our journey. Every moment, the grandeur and toughness of spirit, the seeming treachery of an unformed poem, a renegade thought lassoing and binding itself to our hips, forcing us to work out the unworkable. The voice and imagination of a child is a powerful reflection of our self, our future. Nothing separates you from them, from me, from us—we peel away the layers with fire slipping off our tongues. I write to find out what is happening inside of me—and it's my bridge to understanding the world. My students and the work I did in D.C. WritersCorps were a balm to my spirit. Inside the classroom I learned how to listen, be present in the moment, no matter what my daily lesson plan said. I learned about being human. D.C. WritersCorps was an addiction I had to fill every September for five years. I loved the all-day training sessions and the monthly meetings where 'us' teachers got to catch up on each others' sites, share teaching strategy and ideas—a time to check in and be connected, to know that we were doing something real out in the world and that it had weight and strength.

My site was Stuart Hobson Middle School, and the teacher I worked with, Mrs. Hill, was full of support and wisdom; she was a real champion of the students and their abilities. During my second year of teaching, one of my students wrote a scathing letter to a girl. Once the deed was done and delivered, it began to weigh heavily on him. In an earlier class the students and I had established a sacred place for our writing. We discussed the amazing power of language, how words can be used to hurt or heal—each use with its own set of consequences. By the time the teaching team confronted the young man, he was more than ready to confess and make reparations. He had come to understand the impact of his words and was truly sorry. He was able to put himself in the place of the girl and feel her pain, and it became his pain. It's hard to know just how deeply we affect each other's lives.

Mother I Adore

When my mother walks
away from me, she takes my
sister with her. On

my uncle's farm I learn
the many uses of pig bladders,
intestines, hooves, skin; to wait.

I learn how to take
a kick or a punch without
showing it. Later, I will

push my husband's empty
hands back into the streets.
No one will ever

know who the father
of my first child is even
two children later. And

my fifth grade education
has me cleaning pots and cooking
meals of boiled potatoes,

string beans and fish every
day, waiting. And, later
still, I will take my mother

under my roof when
she is too old, and she will
keep asking about my fast-

tongued sister. And after
I am gone, my granddaughter
will find in the big Bible

 on the coffee table
that my birth date was wrong
and this secret too

will follow me like
the killing of the man and the
changing of our name to

Logan. Fleeing the south
and all its memory . . . .
And if at last I

want to talk
I will be too old to remember
and so I'll leave

hints and promises,
children sitting at windows,
learning how to wait.

Myth

After this, I will float to heaven
like a feather in zero gravity
    —Demetrius Suggs, age 12

In this world of faded grey,
Shades of black-grey and white-grey
and still blacker-grey, I float
under hazy film, static outlines,
ignescent history. I am
an unreliable witness.
Face pressed against time.
Johnson Elementary circa 1936.
All brown-grey bodies, all neat and
tidy for this one snapshot. Frozen.
Crows flutter here, under matte finish.
There's something about the shadows
or something resting in shadow,
weighted, heavy.
I am alone in these smudged faces even
with what we all share.
Right now I float like a penny,

swallowed.
This is me, assembled.
I know what you think you see,
but this is something else,
a children's story,
I am forever,
stolen breath.
I am butcher and burning—
there is the cross,
"sweet jesus" we pray.
These are the things I leave behind.
Our seeds lie scattered.
Remember this

Michele Elliott is co-editor of *D.C. Poets Against the War Anthology*. She taught for many years in the Washington D.C. area: poetry for D.C. WritersCorps, visual art for Corcoran College of Art and Design and playwriting for Woolly Mammoth Theater and Young Playwrights Theater. She holds an M.F.A. in creative writing from the University of Pittsburgh and is a freelance grant writer in Philadelphia.

© Emily Stauffer

Andrew Saito

Writing gave my life purpose and focus after my mother passed away following my junior year of college. I write in order to remember, and to create beauty from suffering. As a poet, I try to craft tributes to concrete, ephemeral moments; as a playwright, I hope to explore and deepen mysteries, and invite audiences to create and engage their own.

Working with WritersCorps was a tremendously fortuitous experience for me. My time encouraging linguistic and literary exploration at Newcomer High School and the San Francisco Public Library exposed me to dozens of distinct voices from disparate global origins, who all were living for a time in the same small city. Above all, these young writers shared individual stories and taught me that youth, regardless of nationality, have wisdom and perspective that deserve an audience.

Playwright Erik Ehn calls writing a charitable act. Teaching writing furthers this service, for teaching artists encourage our students' incubation of talents and passions that feed growth and creation, inviting experience and communication. In teaching literary arts to youth, we endorse their own agency, calling upon them to be responsible for their own choices, both on the page and in the world.

From the play *El Rio*

Scene: REYNALDO MADRID, a Mexican American member of the Border Patrol. (*He is on duty.*)

REYNALDO:
Most people think of the Border Patrol as an all-white organization. Hell, I did before I joined. But that's just not how it works down here. Half us agents have names like Martínez, Pérez, González, Cantú. I'm Madrid. Don't ask if I've ever been to Spain, though. I'm from the Valley. My parents were born here. My grandparents, too. The only family stories from Mexico come from when this land was still Mexico. But the border moved south, so we're Texans now. And I'm proud to be a Texan. Just as there's Mexican pride, there's Texan pride. On this job I can see that huge Mexican flag flapping away across the river. It's like

they're taunting us. All our flags are small. Maybe that's what you get in the land of immigrants. They don't appreciate the stars and stripes. That's not their blood up there.

Scene: BARRY BROWNWATER, a Kickapoo Indian truck driver.

BARRY:
There are too many Mexicans these days. They're invading the reservation. That's why I had to move off. They drove me off. I only speak two languages. Kickapoo, and the white man's tongue. I don't like the white man's tongue. Nothing but lies. And it sounds ugly. But most people don't talk Kickapoo. Over in that reservation, it's Spanish everywhere. No one talks Kickapoo anymore. No one cares about tradition. It's all money. I told them not to put that casino up there. I told them it would bring problems. Casinos. That was Reagan's gift to us Indians. Greed. That's why they ran me off. 'Cause I say my mind. 'Cause I talk Kickapoo. So I went to live in Mexico. That's ceremonial land down there, but I live there all the time, when I'm not on the road. Can't live with that Kansas band. Can't live with that Texas band. Only place to go is Mexico. Only place with any freedom left.

From the play *Greetings From the Klondike . . . Wish You Were Here!*

Scene: IRENE, an older Inupiaq woman.

IRENE:
I used to be beautiful. (*pause*) I was beautiful, and the whole village adored me. Thirty men asked for my hand. Thirty men! I was vain. But I was worth it. And I refused them all. I refused them because they made me vain. They lavished me with gifts. Furs and jewelry. Eggs. One of them even bought me flowers. Tulips. All the way from Europe. He must have used his life savings. But not your father. Do you know what he brought me? (pause) Stones. Every night, he left a stone on my doorstep. He did it for months. He did it for three years! (*pause*) One night, I waited up by the window, to find out who it was. I stayed up so late. But not late enough. My head fell asleep by the window. When I woke up, there was a stone at the other side of the glass. Now, you may not think a stone is anything special. You may think dozens of stones are a burden. I thought so. But after all the suitors came and went, and the eggs were all eaten, and the tulips dried and carried off with

the wind, there was still a stone, every morning, waiting for me. And I knew that this man would be as constant as the stones he left, and I could trust him as I trust the ground the stones come from. (*pause*) After many months, after many stones, I left him a gift. I put a pin made from whale bone in the exact spot where he always left the stone. The next morning, it was gone, a stone sitting in its place. I started searching the village everyday. I knew this man would be the most beautiful man in the whole village. I wanted to find him. I needed to find him! I searched faces. I searched eyes and mouths. But I could not find him. And I lost hope. The stones started to haunt me. I thought they were some curse. They weighed me down. They wanted to crush me. To push the life out of me. They became a constant reminder that I would die, old and unwed. (*pause*) One morning, I went to the beach. I threw all the stones into the ocean. It took me so long to carry them from the house. My arms burned after throwing so many stones into the waves. As I was leaving, something made me stop. There was a man hunched over the ground. I approached him from behind, and asked what he was doing. "Looking for something," he said. He turned around slow, and I saw him: the man with the lame foot. The man who limped, and was too slow to hunt. The man who did women's work, if anyone would even let him. the man who wore old and discarded furs. The man who ate the worst pieces of meat. The man who sucked on bones. The man with no family, who everyone knew, but nobody spoke to. I wanted to run. But I just looked. He put forth his hand, a smooth green stone in his blistered palm, and said, "Your beauty is as eternal as this." I saw the pin, displayed on his jacket for all to see. A week later, we were married.

Andrew Saito has taught in San Francisco with WritersCorps, Performing Arts Workshop and Kearny Street Workshop, and in rural Guatemala through the ArtCorps program. His playwriting has been presented on several stages, including the Magic Theatre, Galería de la Raza, the Off-Market Theatre, Bindlestiff Studio, La Peña Cultural Center and SomArts. In Fall 2008 he began an Iowa Arts Fellowship at the Playwrights Workshop at the University of Iowa.

© Nancy Dymond

Mary "Maya" Hebert

The year I entered WritersCorps, I had just published a children's book. So when I walked into my first after-school program at Mind-Builders Creative Arts Center in the Bronx and looked into the eyes of a dozen seven-to ten-year-olds, I was excited beyond measure. As a writer who had never taught, I also felt a wave of panic.

In WritersCorps, I learned to teach as my Muse had taught me—playing with the energy of natural objects and photographs, and listening for the stories they evoked. When it worked, it felt less like teaching, and more like building a safe and colorful bridge for the poetry of children's thoughts to land.

Listening to children write their dreams and fears week after week opened new places in me. My own poetry took on new life—new sounds and images and heart—as life took on new purpose.

I write to penetrate the surface of things, to find the common thread that connects us. For me, WritersCorps is living proof that writing is vital because it creates community—a *common unity* that lifts us out of the ordinary to touch that true and high part of us.

Moss

We are the uncurling
green miniatures built
on mineral breath
knitting earth
with new desire.

We are the early intelligence
of chlorophyll sprouting from iron.

We are where stone is plenty and damp,
where mounds rise, and wood yields
to non wood

where nothing dies
without becoming.

Day
January 24, 2002
Greenpoint, Brooklyn

It begins in the morning with the seagull run,
their boomerang wings appearing
out of clouds for bits of bread on my roof. Their hunger,
the meagerness of bread for their large bodies,
and a thread starts to unravel. Looking down

I realize my body is filling with shadows of Earth.

Then low-floating clouds swallow the island of Manhattan,
so from my window just the spire of the Chrysler Building
is visible, sticking up awkward as an acupuncture needle
in soft skin. Clouds twist and swirl and swallow that too.

I wonder if I should get on the G train, or if the
53rd Street tunnel will end in a mist. Now I watch

everything for meaning, especially my cat perching
on the table, covering the pink newsprint from London
with black fur, the coiled tales of greed and corruption,
her white nose mask facing east as she watches the
living room where I sometimes perform healings.

I recall the ether kingdom where the flowers know me by name.

I recall we are 38 in a circle, sitting on hay in Western
    Massachusetts,
we have 2 minutes each to share, and one woman says,
It's too hard being human I want to be a tree.

I hold the box of tea like a book and read, "Indulge yourself
in what you do well. Spend time with people who think you're
    splendid."
It's a quote from Victoria Moran. I make a mental list and
    wonder if
I must think I'm splendid to spend time with myself. I put on

my coat for Manhattan. My list says:
new light bulb for desk,
Appleworks software,

new foam mattress,
hair color;
I cross out the mattress.

My cat doesn't want me to leave. I know she sees
things. At the token booth a woman jumps
ahead of me. *People are out for themselves now,* I think.

On the platform a couple in black leather and blue eyes and hair
that needs combing eat a meal on the subway bench as if it's
their last; they are delicate and checking with long fingers
at the bag edge what's left. At Court Square

next to the ads for Rockports and Lotto the posters scream
UNITED WE STAND
I am angry now.
United we stand for what? I am waiting

for the V train that replaced the F at certain stations.
It's part of a master plan to encourage separation,
to keep people in Queens and South Brooklyn farther
apart. At Lex and 53rd the doors open and

chords from an acoustic guitar enter, sit across from me.

At the credit union the cashier is tired and hands me 160 dollars
too much. I hand it back. We are both stunned that this
moment will determine the course of our lives. I am giddy

now half running to 5th Avenue for my ritual
bus ride from the library to 14th Street. Walking through Bryant
Park I listen for remnant waters from the reservoir once here.

At the computer store I nervously plunk down
90 dollars in cash to buy software I'm unsure of, but that will
    make me
compatible. I am no longer giddy. I have already been to Duane
Reade for L'Oreal Colorspa Auburn No. 14 that's actually good
for my hair, and realize I can go home now.

I picture my roof and the seagulls from morning, and feel
the knot at the end of the thread: that we are all creatures

of the grey landscape, and what color feathers might be if this
island
were still blue and green.

I open the door but do not turn on my kitchen light.
I sit for a while and trade breaths with the smoky edges
of what we name the dark.

Mary "Maya" Hebert is the author of the poetry book *My Father's Window*
(Rain Mountain Press) and the children's book *Horatio Rides the Wind* (Tem-
plar Publishing, London; and Koala Books, Australia). She has been awarded
writer's residencies at the Tyrone Guthrie Center in Ireland, Dorset Colony
in Vermont and the Ragdale Foundation in Illinois.

JoNelle Toriseva

Placing words on a page, constructing sentences to enter and exit worlds, is a great privilege and pleasure. I wrote my first book when I was ten, and I've been writing ever since. I was one of the original San Francisco WritersCorps members—and I have the T-shirt to prove it! WritersCorps was amazing.

The writers I worked with inspired me—both the other Corps members and the youth I taught at International Studies Academy, Everett Middle School, Newcomer High School and in one of those temporary trailer classrooms parked one block north of Mission and 16th Street. All of these students enriched my life through their insight, their passion and their sheer nerve. We created, we cried, we honored our experiences. We traveled to real and imagined places and made more space for ourselves in the world.

For me writing has been a way to deepen my relationship with the world and with other people. Writing gives meaning to my experiences, and to our shared experiences in life. It was a privilege and an honor to journey through writing with youth during my WritersCorps tenure. My phenomenal students taught me so much about standing full in my honesty and keeping true to myself. Every day they came to school with such courage—and worked so hard. Fifteen years later, I salute them, wherever they are. And I salute you, all you writers out there. Write on!

From the novel *The House Of Dandelion*

Dandelion Rites

On the stock pond behind my brother and I, the ice cracks. The thaw lodges the wagon wheels deeper into the half frozen mud as we load feed. Even though it's April, unexpectedly, the wind melts the snow around us.

The crows reel around the silage pile. Flying low over the top, a cardinal suddenly drops and flies into the dun colored side. The silage, solidly frozen through the long winter, ferments in the warm spring air. The smell unleashes the air around us. I have been avoiding my brother through the entire feeding, stepping out of his way, walking backwards around him. If I can get through the chores I will be fine.

Black clods of dirt and angled white ax heads of snow melted to ice rake the field. Black. White. Black. White. Gray. The deep shadows of the poplar trees lining the south side scrape the snow banks shaded from the sun. The sun marks the sky purple and apricot.

I push the large round hay bale, rolling off one layer of hay at a time. Stamping down the hay under my feet, the round becomes smaller as I unwind it. Behind me, my mother and father, heads bent down in front, spread the hay wide with their pitchforks. The cows push in to eat. My mother and father have disappeared from my view. I sidestep a Black Angus mother and calf and for an instant forget to guard myself.

My brother's hand comes down like a hatchet. My nose deflates. "Pa, Pa!" I cry.

The sleeve of Pa's torn red sweatshirt opens in the wind. He rests on the pitchfork, squinting at my black-haired brother and then at me. Then, he spears his fork into the crust on the silage pile and heaves out a square. A cry breaks out of the center of my throat.

"Behave, Em." Pa clears his throat, smelling the wind like a cinnamon bear.

Em glares at me, and pulls the hood off his head, biting the safety pin on the end of the shoelace tie. I feel like I am holding a brown egg whole in my mouth.

I should stop, right? I should reverse. I should roll up all the dried alfalfa again, with myself in the middle, safe from my brother. But, it is too late. We are on to the next part of the feeding.

After tossing silage on the pile, Pa swings and gouges Em's shoulder with the wooden end of the fork. Em turns around and stares at me. Catching Pa's eye, Em, eyes flashing like a Blue Jay, hits at me again. This time the hatchet hits frozen ground. Looking down, I taste copper and watch the blood bore small round holes, like BB shot scattered in snow.

Mom, with hands like the pine stacked on the woodpile, looks away. Doesn't see it now, didn't see it the first time. She leans down and dislodges the knitted green scarf wound around her neck. Looking at the three of them, my thoughts wind down smaller and smaller, curving into a snail shell. Mom walks to the gate. I walk after her, but she climbs onto the tractor and starts it up before I can get on the back. The planks of the flat trailer jostle behind her, dirt and rocks scramble off. As she drives the tractor close to the silage pile, I finally make the jump onto the wagon. I climb on the wagon, balancing with my feet on two of the loose boards, bending my knees with the jolts.

Riding the wagon I can see the crest of the hill, the place where I wait for the school bus with Emmett. I can see the yellow ghost of it almost there. The bus will be there Monday. It is always Monday here. It is always chore time. It is always Emmett aiming things at me. Emmett attempting to sever my head from my thighs, my calves from my forearms, my knees from my hands, my elbows from my feet.

Here it doesn't change. It will not change. Standing on the back of the wagon, I become half crow, half girl. I do say goodbye, but the chugging of the tractor is louder than my voice.

Head tilted back, I walk past the Black Angus bull, through the small bales that need stacking, past the heifers waiting for their oats, past the woodpile, around the doghouse. Calico cat rubbing around my ankles. As I turn right onto the gravel road, the pull on my belly, like the shock of an electric fence, hits me as I cross the boundaries of their sight. Rubber soled boots sliding in the mud, I am gone, out without telling anyone where.

My feet hit the staccato of corn stubble as I cut across the field. When I pass the line of Quaking Aspen that marks our land, I shudder only slightly. A small left-over sort of jolt and I am off our property.

I do not know it yet, though the wild tingle should tell me, that unpredictable current of spring melting winter; but this is the last time I am going to allow my brother to hit me. Though I'm not stronger than him, I can be fast and most of all, I will be mean back. Not mean first, but meanness will be met with meanness in equal measure. After today, I know fairness is not showing its cupped hands around this pole barn or shackle shed with the paint worn to wood. The air around me hums with bare branches. When I am three miles gone from my chores, the brown egg dissolves and I begin breathing.

Dandelion sits on the wet, wooden front steps of her house. Gliding down the icy sidewalk, I almost run into her, skidding to a stop at the last moment possible. She laughs at my chore clothes—my rawhide mitten and my yellow glove, my brother's old tan corduroy jacket.

"Right Whales, Rorquals, Gray Whale, Beaked Whales, Sp—" Dandelion recites the list of California mammals backwards.

"You've never been—" my breath comes out in big puffs in front of me. The sun leaves the long shadow of the yard pole light on us. Even out here, I can smell the steadiness of the cigarettes we've watched her mother smoking with the moon, late at night.

Dandelion's words appear like short sips of clouds, "Mattie, you know me. I like to be prepared."

Moving over to make room on the cardboard box she has folded into an accordion cushion, she hands me the tiny leopard coat I've seen on her sister's Barbie.

"It's fake?" I'm asking myself, but it comes out loud. "Let's walk to town."

She rolls her eyes. It's her decision, her Mom's not home from work so there's no one to know, no one with whom she must bargain. When she stands up, I holler.

Holding hands, navigating over the barely frozen puddles, avoiding branches and a once silver, now burnt-out pick-up, we swing our arms all the way down the driveway.

Somehow, we are prepared for this. I feel it in my legs, as I slide toward the mailbox and look back at Dandelion, laughing. She begins singing. Her voice skitters over the barbed wire and sits in the shadows of the fence posts.

In the ditches where now only the tops of the brush and the smaller pine trees that the deer haven't eaten, poke out of the grey snow; cowslips and wild roses and even ladyslippers will grow. Soon.

Town is seven miles away. We could get there if we wanted. The sun glares off the ice. We walk until we stand under the white pine, made fragrant by the sun.

"You know, I just don't feel like going to town today," I say.

Dandelion shrugs her shoulders. Turning around, the light catches the back of our heads. Light so cold it turns the air into ice, making our breath solid for the moment.

"We could have made it to town."

Dandelion nods, "Easy."

JoNelle Toriseva is the author of two books for children: *Rodeo Day* (Macmillan) and *Becoming Ballet* (Simon & Schuster). Her plays have been produced at the Exit Theatre and Mills College where she earned an M.F.A. in creative writing. She edited *Dust And Fire*, a national anthology of women's writing, and *New Voices*, an anthology of youth writing. Her work is included in *Best Canadian Poetry 2008*. She has taught at Mills College, Universidad del Valle in Guatemala City, California Poets in the Schools and San Francisco Writers-Corps.

Barbara Schaefer

My work in various art forms—dance, choreography, theater, poetry and music—has informed and enhanced my primary work as a visual artist. The interrelationship of these disciplines develops my awareness of the underlying principles that are essential in all art forms. To begin with, all art forms require presence and patience, showing up for the work, even when nothing is apparently happening. Listening, observation, decisiveness, but also release is necessary for the creative process. Art is not separate from growth as a human being and is often frightening and painful, which above all requires courage and taking risks.

I write every morning, for writing allows me to recognize what's below the surface of my mind. The actual act of writing reassembles the parts of myself that have become disassociated. Painting and making music evoke and indicate, but words are more specific and have an exacting power in them. Color, space, sound, silence and movement come alive with words and emerge from the same intuitive process of discovery as every art form does. Being an interdisciplinary artist satisfies these needs.

After living in Rome for twelve years, WritersCorps was my first employment in the United States. When I went to the Bronx for the first time I was shocked by the difference in cultures and what I perceived as a lack of beauty. After the softness of Rome I wasn't sure I would be able to handle teaching in this environment. WritersCorps assigned me to teach poetry in a senior center, which turned out to be—despite my trepidation—a rewarding and inspiring experience for me as well as my students. My role as teacher has more to do with presence than teaching. I act as facilitator to allow my students space and freedom to find words, their own words, for what they may have never expressed. I always begin class with what is there, with what thoughts, feelings or ideas are in the room. From there, worlds unfold and the atmosphere becomes charged and alive. My senior group wrote amazing poems that inspired and moved me and confirmed that you are never too old to write.

The Visit

I've been reading so much about God
that he came into my living room last night
and laid down on my couch with his feet up.
When I asked him about the TRUTH
he laughed
and took out pictures of his sons.
They were all women
with attachable beards.

Suddenly they appeared
and we drank from his palms
drunk with laughter
he came down
from his throne
and took off his disguise.

Shedding Skins

I

I once told Aaron that
I was like a snake
shedding skins,
getting closer to my essence.

He laughed and said
there would always be another
skin to shed.

II

Even before the stroke
my Mother
was tearing off her clothes
in bed.

After the stroke
left her right side paralyzed,

I'd find her stark
naked, pulling at her skin
as though it too was a layer of clothing
she wanted to rip off.

She didn't know why,
she said she was not hot
nor did she forget
I was her daughter
who played the piano,
or that all her money was gone.

III

Unconsciously
we undress for death
and leave nothing behind

Barbara Schaefer is an interdisciplinary artist whose paintings are exhibited internationally. She holds a B.F.A. from the University of Arizona and an M.F.A. from San Francisco State University. She won a Helene Wurlitzer Foundation Artist-in-Residency award in 1997, the New York Foundation For The Arts Sponsorship in 1996, a grant from the Robert Rauschenberg Foundation in 2004 and an Artist-in-Residency award at the Fundación Valparaiso in 2005.

Peter Money

When I was seven I'd write poems and keep them in a toy safe. It was clear to me from early on that poetry was the language that fulfilled my coming of age, that told me I was here. Poetry has always constituted my primary interaction with the world; it seems at once a shout and a whisper.

If writers identify with people to communicate with them, a writer as a teacher must apply that sympathy and teach through it to the empathy of felt experience. We know what the student feels because we have felt it. My time with students, my WritersCorps experience, also made me become, years later, a better parent.

I owe my best listening to Kalani, one of the students at my Writers-Corps site. "I don't want to do this," Kalani said, and in the seconds and minutes that passed I stayed with him to hear his own answer liberate a space that had previously seemed confining. Kalani breathed out an honesty of experience that adults commonly pass over: "Blue, just blue"—and then, "Holy shoots! I'm seeing something." While looking at the sky from the asphalt playground together, Kalani relayed to me his direct observation, a spontaneous exhortation which felt, I remember, profound to both of us—a rush of images compelled him: "a volcano, God, UFOs, George Washington, stars, the moon, shatterings, clouds, a bird, Golden Gate Park, sun"—and suddenly, a memory of his own grandmother's voice: "just be good as gold,/ be nice, don't drink and drive,/ don't lie." My teacher, Ginsberg, and his friend Kerouac said similar things as advice to writers; Kalani was not alone with his grandmother's words.

But the gold is where we are, even if it seems to be taking its time. Maybe taking our time *is* the gold—a lesson poetry offers but which time does not always permit. If I am a better parent—if!—I am probably a teacher with reason, a citizen of emotions and a writer for ever widening consciousness. I would hope leaders and teachers will bring to the world a candor and honor that reveres our time here, and prepares the space for others. We are a circle of others.

From *To Day — Minutes Only: A Poetry Correspondence With Exiled Poet Saadi Yousef*

I began corresponding with Iraqi exile writer Saadi Yousef half a year before the U.S. invaded his homeland. The sequence that followed was a call and response I hadn't expected. The excerpt, below, is from my recent book To Day—Minutes Only which is a prose-poem "dialog piece" using my correspondence and contact with Saadi Yousef (also "Youssef"). This was my small-part-of-the-world attempt to Stop War. The sequence was part of an effort to "put a human face" on Iraq—as if the human faces could not be seen. I thought an American poet, particularly one now "sequestered" in the hills of Vermont, ought to know an Iraqi poet.

September 01 you were writing "That rainy day," September 01, twelfth day, I was looking out toward this mountain—thinking about the many hands which made Giza. September 02 I found you among dozens (you stood out—as if fastened to the paper, a circumstance which would not disappear) . . . you and Abdel Wahabal-Bayati, Bulandal Haydari, Mohammed Mahdial-Jawahiri: poets of the road: strength (maybe?) in the stream of characters making us waves of ancestors; take that character, Aboud: Hamlet— no complainer but a teller of time—(wandering everywhere a skull has to go).

. . . you carry these things with you, clouds fill your pockets, rain sends their message, light, sparrows resting then bending the stalk; the answer is unexpected, even now: where will it come from? . . . And how often did we feel a tug at our sleeve?—this way, that. here now.

So much had they to say they were feared for their freedom.

in the distance flowers and headstones are quenching their thirst / I wrote to you because I was lost. . . / *pores open to the music.* / And now Ginsberg: . . . "Aunt Rose, now might I see you . . . " "in this extremely strange situation together"—dead or alive, a sentience no sentence may reduce: except to a word, by the living or the dead, we read in every language.

This question is the world's—and I'm afraid who will answer will not be the painter, no composer, no lover, dancer—

but a dictator's (without imagination), a profiteer, a lark
without conscience, obliterator . . .

Minutes only and I shall make with your love a narrow bed.

Snow, Saadi, nothing but snow, falling; ash, you could say,
but for the tongue, thirsting & for the branch
—a shared sky, renewal by these multifold stories;
& now I cannot look at snow the same way: you in Amman
(I had no idea . . .), a flake on your shoulder, you looked up. Here,
we put aside our work & global position. . . & look up,
out, across, into the eyes of snow—& hear a thousand voices,
falling. And feel their, as you say, shiver.

I feel them shiver.

the sun has dwelt in the books of travelers and poets / Just this
little bit, if I may help (I was a waiter once, here, this cup of water)—
& now, always a new day, the sky fills: peach, pink, human
—to human, as I walk up the icy hill with two small children.

. . . smoke curls backward as if a word upon itself, rising only
with wind, dissipating—the blue sweeps upward, leading the eye
above; and now there is no difference between smoke and cloud.
O, how it came to night. In the sky: ash. On the ground: more

snow. And when sleep should have me: instead I find myself
in a café, communicating alone—a chair by a window,
a light—far off . . . an elderly man wrapped in white & smoking
a pipe stared at me, stares still. By day the color is flaked skin,
the taste is dust, the sound is nothing
but once in a while a breeze wrapping around a tree; a motorcycle
or swift small car is the only passing action. I feel I am beginning
to understand what exile will be—

Stars, Saadi, as much as a single word, we translate into being,
as little light as night illumines—a modest tree
on the snowy field, its moonshadow, a huge lung,
breathing—

Earth is left, and we—we figure the minutes to day.

Silence. This writing . . . the children asleep. The green—bottle

—a mountain for a stem. You said (Youssef) "Ashjar"
—for tree—while I was turning a log in our fireplace! In my place
parts of trees turn to ash; and poetry's jar—empty or with ash,
vessel for fire, firefly, a fuel to this, food—hands.
And we seem closer than ever: Compeled to cradle the life
even while fingers still hold ash. These ember.
(Can I say today, God willing?)—or, will the willing set fire to
ephemeral things, flood the page, to prison the pen?
(How much should we tend versus wait?) To what extent
must one pray? Pay attention?) By poetry we mediate & meditate
. . . & "away from us snow is filling its basket"— / this.

 may they feel it upon them now.

*

may they feel it upon them now.

Peter Money is the editor of Harbor Mountain Press. His poetry books in-
clude *These Are My Shoes*, *Finding It: Selected Poems* and *To Day—Minutes Only*.
He has also recorded the spoken word CD *Blue Square*. He teaches at The
Center For Cartoon Studies and has been the chair of the creative writing
and literature department at Lebanon College in New Hampshire. His work
has been heard on NPR's *The Writer's Almanac* and has been published inter-
nationally, including in *The American Poetry Review* and *Talisman*.

© Katharine Gin

Cindy Je

Most of my poems are sparked by personal history, by family stories and issues my family never talked about. I am the person I am in part because of decisions I had no part in. This fascinates me to no end. Before I was born, my grandfather disappeared for two years and my father wasn't able to graduate from college because he had to take care of my grandmother and his five younger sisters. Because of these events I write in English.

I am a person straddling many worlds, living a hybrid life by trying to balance language, art, education, communities and resources. I come from a place of enormous privilege but only half a generation away from poverty. I grew up in Orange County with the requisite big house and swimming pool because my parents worked seven days a week for over ten years without vacation time or sick days. While my parents were at work, my grandparents took care of my siblings and me. Every once in a while we'd hear a story about how in Korea they were too poor to buy shoes and how they had to eat a lot of Spam. These stories were strange and felt surreal because I didn't realize that not having shoes meant not being able to walk to school, and my dad actually liked Spam. I identify as Korean American but have lost much of my Korean tongue. The words take so long to form in my mouth and my accent is off. All this makes me neurotic and somewhat uncomfortable—yet keeps me engaged.

WritersCorps arrived at a crucial time in my life. I could not have had a better first year working at Mission High School and the San Francisco Main Library in the 2007 to 2008 school year. My students didn't all want to be writers but they were willing to challenge themselves. They helped me to realize how language is a key part of feeling empowered, and they inspired me with their stories. Almost all of my students had a job and a few of my students went to school all day and went to work in a crummy job from nine at night to seven in the morning. There is nothing like walking into a classroom and having twenty people turn to you with big smiles and ask how you're doing. It's humbling and energizing.

My own writing teachers taught me how important it is to know you have a voice and that individual voices and lives matter. The act of writing affirms a right to exist, be heard and make a distinct mark. I am privileged to be in a position to try to pass this on.

How the Angels of Light Reach Your Eye

The fleas and the lice—
and next to my pillow,
a pissing horse
        —Basho

It's been raining for three weeks
and for the first time in four years,
I realize I'm living in a valley.

The outline of sunlight is clear—
I count five brown mountain ranges,
the distant star pines across the river
unveiled from the yellowed
wallpaper of smog.

Beyond the pale brick classrooms,
I squish through spongy grass
and mud, afraid of my own voice
dissolving into the steam clouds
rising beneath my feet,
misting my vision in water and salt.

Beside the bell tower,
two architecture students argue
about the validity of Christ
as a carpenter because he never
built a house or a tool shed.
I don't look back.

Maybe the students gesture
with the longing for words as old mountain gods,
not knowing how angels
structure such perfect raindrops
or how fleas and lice live off skin and blood.

I'm reading Basho's *The Narrow Road to the Interior*,
a poetic saint's travel diary
where no one fears
long poems or obscurity,

it seems,
yet Sora's diary records Basho's desires
for the national prominence and affluence
of a new black horse.

All that we can leave behind
is someone else's

memory of ourselves or our words.
Maybe my life is without the foundation
of even a rice paper boat.

And so in the gray fading light
with the chirping of crickets,
all I can do is kneel
through the water and salt.

The Seams

Outside my window—
    each wet leaf is still.
The clothes I've taken
off, an ash gray pile
on the floor.
    I try to remember
the first day of losing,

I look at the dark curve
below each inner elbow,
    a shallow slit
inherited from my mother's side.
I look to remind me of the surrender
of desire,
how body becomes ghost.

    How much I want
to give back to my body . . .
The pink tongue
and ear of secrets slipping—
    my mother sending off
        dreams of sewing red dresses;

my grandmother burning
    her best dress and jacket
to clothe a death,
    the pale spirit of my aunt.

I waited three months
for her return
in that dress
but tasted dirty ashes.

I embroidered an apricot
    tree on my pillow, the cross-
stitches of leaves catch the fears

I will fill.
I slip on my dress,
the seams slide
    down my arms and settle
on my shoulders
like rain.

A Sign of Blessing

In the lace
of fog and lamplight,
maybe you were
meant to step off
the gray curb while gazing
towards the Seine. Your step
fighting gravity,
unlike the ghostly statues
dancing upon L'Hôtel de Ville.

The mystery of the space
between your red shoes
and the speeding yellow Fiat.

You weren't frightened.
Your Aunt Clare anticipated this
when you were seven years old
that third week in July

when you tried to touch the flaming window.
She slapped you
across your face, a strike
meant to hold you
in the violent arm of grace.

The driver
and his three passengers
turned back
with eyebrows and mouths traced
in amazement
and with frantic hands offered
to buy you a cup of coffee.

You were saved.
You stood stunned—
one step off the curb,
before the open window,
two inches before
tentatively
touching it
like St. Thomas
placing his finger
into the wound.

Cindy Je was born in Korea and moved to the U.S. as a child. She earned her M.F.A. in creative writing at the University of Oregon and her B.A. at U.C. Riverside, where she was awarded the Roy T. Thompson Poetry Award and the Ina Coolbrith Memorial Prize. She is an education specialist for A Home Away From Homelessness and has taught writing at the middle school, high school and university level. She joined San Francisco WritersCorps in 2007.

Chad Sweeney

I served in San Francisco WritersCorps for seven years at Mission High School, Mercy Housing and Everett Middle School. Most of my students were newly arrived teenagers from Central America, East Asia or the Middle East. Their writing reflected a sense of isolation and loss, but also of hope and curiosity. One student hid under melons to cross the U.S. border, while many walked from as far as Guatemala through deserts and cities. A young woman from Yemen entered school for the first time at the age of eighteen, determined to master English, and wrote during her first month, "I am the Arabian horse, the red inside the white." Each day was a rich cultural exchange for us, a chance to stretch beyond ourselves and to know ourselves more truly. Poetry allowed for play and freedom among the students, but also for vigorous investigation and critical thinking within a stimulating group dynamic. I think we've only begun to scratch the surface of what creative writing can accomplish in an educational setting.

In my own life as well, poetry is a coming into knowledge, an awakening to sensory experience—to the broken glass, salt spray and irises—as well as an inner-guide to the unconscious and to the collective memory buried in Story. Poetry integrates the disconnected parts of the self, bringing the humours into balance, reconciling opposing urgencies or leaving those urgencies poised in dramatic tension—a tension which, in the eye of an artist, is pleasure and a deeper truth. Like a mathematics of bicycle tires and light, poetry makes use of any materials—a crow feather, a memory, an earthquake. The joy of my life has been in wandering the mountains, the dunes, or the back alleys of a city, a buddhist temple in Tibet, a mosque in Palestine, or an immigration rally in San Francisco, and touching these scenes by writing about them, as if language were the sixth sense—or the first sense. Working with WritersCorps youth has held me close to that first sense, to the source of our shared inheritance as human beings.

The Piano Teacher

A music box wound too tightly will explode,
playing its song all at once.
The practice is to unwind the song slowly.
Think of this when you touch the key of C.

A black hole warbles the note *B flat*
in waves as wide as galaxies
forty octaves below your house.
Think of this when you love someone.

Sound has its own horizon.
Our meetings will happen there.
The cello is floating away.
The ribs of a tiger are rippling.

Chad Sweeney's poetry books include *Arranging The Blaze* (Anhinga), *An Architecture* (BlazeVox) and *A Mirror To Shatter The Hammer* (Tarpaulin Sky). He is co-editor of the literary journal *Parthenon West Review*, and his poems and translations have appeared widely, including in *The Best American Poetry 2008*, *Crazyhorse, Colorado Review, New American Writing* and *Verse Magazine*. He studies poetry and English literature in the Ph.D. program at Western Michigan University.

Acknowledgments

Grateful acknowledgment is made to the publications in which these works have previously been published. Unless specifically noted otherwise, copyright to the works is held by the individual writers.

Ellis Avery: From *The Teahouse Fire* by Ellis Avery, copyright © 2006 by Ellis Avery. Used by permission of Riverhead Books, an imprint of Penguin Group (USA) Inc.

Stephen Beachy: "No Time Flat" from *Some Phantom/No Time Flat* by Stephen Beachy, copyright © 2006 by Stephen Beachy. First published by Three Roads Press/Suspect Thoughts Press.

Thomas Centolella: "Transparency" and "Setsubun" from *Terra Firma* by Thomas Centolella, copyright © 1990 by Thomas Centolella. First published by Copper Canyon Press.

Paola Corso: "Step by Step with the Laundress" appeared in *Subtropics*.

Aja Couchois Duncan: "In Situ" appeared in *Tinfish*.

Mahru Elahi: "Thea," "Robert," "Annie," "Eric," and "Jessica" from *Riding Rough Roads Really Slow* by Mahru Elahi, copyright © 2007 by Mahru Elahi.

Kathy Evans: "Juvenile Hall" appeared in *Americas Review*.

Mary "Maya" Hebert: "Day" appeared in *Skidrow Penthouse*.

Livia Kent: "Mother Tongues: A Memoir" appeared in *Roux*.

Michelle Matz: "The Pear Tree" appeared in *So To Speak*. "Ars Poetica" appeared in *Limestone*. "Pieces" appeared in *Berkeley Poetry Review*.

Jeffrey McDaniel: "Day 4305" from *The Endarkenment* by Jeffrey McDaniel, copyright © 2008 by Jeffrey McDaniel. Reprinted by permission of the University of Pittsburgh Press. "The Offer" from *Alibi School*, by Jeffrey McDaniel, copyright © 1995 by Jeffrey McDaniel.

D. Scot Miller: "Post-Apocalyptic Blues" and "Revisited" appeared in *Nocturnes (Re)view*.

Maiana Minahal: "You Bring Out the Filipina in Me" appeared in *Screaming Monkeys*, edited by M. Evelina Galang. Published by Coffee House Press.

Peter Money: "To Day—Minutes Only: A Poetry Correspondence with Exlied Poet Saadi Yousef" from *To Day—Minutes Only* by Peter Money, copyright by Peter Money. Published by Goats and Compasses Press. Excerpts also appeared in *Art/Life*, web de So's *In Posse*, *Chiron Review* and *Blue Square* (Pax Recordings).

Hoa Nguyen: "Add Some Blue" from *Add Some* Blue by Hoa Nguyen, copyright © 2004 by Hoa Nguyen. First published by Backwoods Broadsides.

Ishle Yi Park: "Jejudo Dreams" and "Railroad" from *The Temperature of This Water* by Ishle Yi Park, copyright © 2004 by Ishle Yi Park. First published by Kaya Press.

Will Power: From *FLOW* by Will Power, copyright by Will Power.

Christopher Sindt: "Beginning With a Line by Julia Kristeva" appeared in *Nocturnes (Re)view*. "Words For Moving Water" appeared in *Notre Dame Review*.

Chad Sweeney: "The Piano Teacher" from *A Mirror to Shatter the Hammer* by Chad Sweeney, copyright © 2006 by Chad Sweeney. Published by Tarpaulin Sky Press. First appeared in *Black Warrior Review*.

Melissa Tuckey: "Re: The Acquittal of Salvadorian Generals" appeared in *Burgeon: Journal of Dance*. "Portrait of Mona Lisa in Palestine" appeared in *Poets for Palestine,* edited by Remi Kanazi. Published by Al Jisser Group.

San Francisco WritersCorps

Chrissy Anderson-Zavala
Cathy Arellano
Ellis Avery
Alegria Barclay
Stephen Beachy
Cherie Bombadier
Godhuli Bose
Thomas Centolella
Carrie Chang
Elizabeth Chavez
Justin Chin
Eric Chow
Jorge Cortinas
Leslie Davis
Colette DeDonato
Victor Diaz
Aja Couchois Duncan
Rebekah Eisenberg
Mahru Elahi
Ananda Esteva
Kathy Evans
Sauda Garrett
Russell Gonzaga
Aracely Gonzalez
Toussaint Haki
Susanna Hall

Myron Michael Hardy
Donna Ho
Le Hubbard
Cindy Je
Uchechi Kalu
Carrie Kartman
Melissa Klein
Katherine LeRoy
Melissa Lozano
Jaime Lujan
Margot Lynn
Michelle Matz
Scott Meltsner
Elizabeth Meyer
D. Scott Miller
Maiana Minahal
Peter Money
Dani Montgomery
Kim Nelson
Hoa Nguyen
Sharon O'Brien
Milta Ortiz
Beto Palomar
Ishle Park
Steve Parks
Andrew Pearson

Elissa Perry
Michelle Phillips
marcos ramírez
Christina Ramos
Karla Robinson
Victoria Rosales
Yiskah Rosenfeld
Andrew Saito
Jime Salcedo-Malo
Johnna Schmidt
Margaret Schulze
Alison Seevak
Christopher Sindt
giovanni singleton
Chad Sweeney
Luis Syquia
Peter Tamaribuchi
JoNelle Toriseva
Elsie Washington
Chris West
Marvin White
Canon Wing
Will Wylie
Gloria Yamato
Tara Youngblood

Bronx WritersCorps

Frank Abporu
Tamara Adams
Andre Alexander
Frank Algarin
Andrew Leman Anderson
Lucy Aponte
Allison Blount
Patricia Blount
Llise Bomen
Coleen Booth
Gamal Abdel Chasten
Edward Clapp
Anthony Darryl Davis
Carlos Diaz
Darlene Gold

Bobby Gonzales
Suheer Hammad
Jennifer Jazz
Victor Larell
Earl Majette
Mariposa
Thea Martinez
Sarah McCarthy
Carthrin McDonnell
Jesus Papoleto Mendez
Tiffany Miller
Flaco Navaya
Geoffrey Nuah
Pedro Pacheco
Azekuna Porideve

Juan Gomez Quroz
Ana Ramos
Hector Rivera
John Rodriguez
Jessica Roman
Nellie Rosario
Alba Sanchez
Caya Schaan
Barbara Schaefer
George Edward Tait
Becca Welfson
Elizabeth Werner
Edgar Nkosi White

D.C. WritersCorps

D.C. WritersCorps thanks all the teaching artists who have served the youth of D.C.